Hebrews Through New Eyes

Christ and His Rivals

Douglas Wilson

Athanasius Press

Monroe, Louisiana

Hebrews Through New Eyes: Christ and His Rivals

205 Roselawn
Monroe, Louisiana 71201
www.athanasiuspress.org

Contents

Part One | An Orientation to Hebrews

Part Two | Commentary on Hebrews

Part One

An Orientation to Hebrews

1

Learning to Type

It has long been an adage among public speakers that one should tell the audience what he is going to tell them, then tell them, and conclude by telling them what he told them. This invigorating advice I intend to follow, in part because seeing the Bible "through new eyes" is very difficult if we have been accustomed to read it in other ways. Repetition is not harmful, and in many cases very helpful (Phil. 3:1).

I therefore want to anticipate some of the great themes of Hebrews before we go through the book passage by passage. But in order to do that, we need to begin by considering the business of types and antitypes.

The Word of God comes to us in many ways, with multiple figures and devices. We are comfortable with many of them, and not quite so comfortable with others. One of the areas of discomfort is the biblical practice of using types and antitypes. This is not just a literary device of God as he inspired the Scriptures to be written—it is also a literary device of his in the writing of the actual history of our world. We must be careful, of course, because "fanciful" interpretations are always a danger. But, if we are honest, we must recognize that many *scriptural* interpretations would strike us as fanciful if they weren't in the Bible. Not only that, but many sober attempts to stick close to the exegetical shore are not really sober at all—sticking close to shore when the text calls us out to sea is not really "playing it safe." The whole idea of playing it safe needs to be treated with wisdom. The fellow who buried his one talent in the ground was playing it safe, which is why he was taking such a huge risk. And the master praised those who risked what he had given them and were therefore playing it safe as well.

Returning to the image of sticking close to the shore, we should not even imagine that we know what the shore *is* apart from what Scripture teaches us. Of course we want to be "safe," if by that we mean under the pleasure of God. And if we want to study our Bibles under the pleasure of God, we should not bring to the text certain *a priori* assumptions about what God can and cannot tell us, as well as assumptions about the ways in which he is permitted to tell us. We must learn from Scripture how to handle Scripture.

And so this is an area where we must be willing to grow. The imagination must not be flighty—it must be disciplined by the Scriptures and by the mind of Christ. And as we are taught by Scripture, we should not be surprised when we learn some things we were not expecting to learn.

"... putting everything in subjection under his feet."

> Now in putting everything in subjection to him, he left nothing outside his control. At present, we do not yet see everything in subjection to him. But we see him . . . (Heb. 2:8–9a)

The author of Hebrews has just cited Psalm 8, where David was amazed that God even *cares* for man, and that God has placed everything (in principle) under man's feet. When God did this, the writer maintained that nothing was excluded from this grant—everything in the world was placed under the authority of man (v. 8). Nevertheless there was just a little hitch—man appeared to lack the kind of authority and control over all things that the psalm seemed to promise him. We do not yet *see* all things subject to him (v. 8). Yes, that is true, but we do see *Jesus* (v. 9). Now we can only see Jesus at the center of the world, at the center of the promises, at the center of the Old Testament, if we take care to see a certain way *in faith*. Jesus Christ is not visible to the eye of unbelief, and Jesus is not visible to the eye of modernity's demand for their idea of proof, which really amounts to unbelief.

In order to see Jesus in this way, there are certain prerequisites. First, we must understand the total, complete, and exhaustive sovereignty of God. If God is not driving the car, we cannot ask him where he is taking us. Second, we must have absolute confidence in the Bible as the Word of God. This means, among many other things, that we must allow the Bible to teach us how to read the Bible. Adam was a *type* of Christ (Rom. 5:14). Israel in the wilderness was a *type* of the church (1 Cor. 10:6). The earthly tabernacle was built according to a *type* of the heavenly tabernacle that was shown to Moses on the mountain (Heb. 8:5). The earthly holy places are the *antitype* of the heavenly places (Heb. 9:24). Christian baptism is the *antitype* of Noah's flood (1 Pet. 3:21). These things are not numinous anomalies in an otherwise ordinary world—they are ordinary mountain peaks in an ordinary world. This is the way the whole terrain works. Some parts of the terrain are more obvious than others, but the whole terrain is connected.

And last, we must know that God has exalted Jesus to the very highest place, such that it is appropriate for us to believe that everything is somehow, in some way, about him (Phil. 2:9; Col. 1:18). Neither type nor antitype is necessarily "senior." Just think of them answering to one another, as deep calls to deep.

So let's take a few examples of this from the book of Hebrews. We have already noted that Paul teaches that a *type/antitype* relationship exists between Israel in the wilderness and the church in *her* wilderness period—between the resurrection of Jesus and the destruction of the temple. Paul is explicit about it. "Now these things happened to them as an example [lit. *tupos*, type], but they were written down for our instruction, on whom the end of the ages has come" (1 Cor. 10:11).

Paul is not talking about the end of the space/time continuum here, but rather about the end of the Judaic aeon. Just as Israel spent forty years in the wilderness before she invaded Canaan, so the church spent forty years in her wilderness before she invaded the world.

This typological parallel is also made very plain in Hebrews (3:7–4:11). The children of Israel hardened their hearts during their wilderness experience. God rebuked them for it in Psalm 95—do not harden your hearts as you did in the wilderness. Then this warning is cited by the author of Hebrews and applied to his readers in *their* peculiar situation (Heb. 4:3). During this forty-year period, God's Word was delivered to both groups on the verge of a great invasion. Some were faithful like Joshua and Caleb. Some were not. In the New Covenant, the people of God faced the same challenges that had been faced by the Jews in the Old Covenant. The difference was, with the resurrection of Christ, long-term success was promised and guaranteed. But that did not mean that this success was going to occur apart from means. The challenges were still the same, the temptations the same, the opportunities for individuals to apostatize were the same, and hence the warnings were the same. We will miss one of the central points of Hebrews if we miss this—the warnings are genuine warnings.

Another example of typological argument in Hebrews is found in the mysterious character of Melchizedek. Hebrews tells us that Christ was a priest after the order of Melchizedek (Heb. 5:6). But *how*? Melchizedek was an obscure king/priest mentioned briefly in the book of Genesis, and then fleetingly in Psalm 110. The whole argument for the Melchizedekan priesthood of Jesus is typological. If we exclude typological reasoning, about the only fact we have is that Jesus was *not* from the tribe of Levi, and I cannot conceive of any non-typological argument that could be developed from that. Here are the assumptions: the Old Testament is talking about Jesus

(5:6, 10); that he was great enough for Abraham to tithe to (7:2, 4–6); etymological considerations of his name and the name of his city (7:2); no recorded genealogy (7:3). Christ was in the *likeness* of Melchizedek (7:15). If we meditate on this for a moment, it should really bring us up short. We want the writer of Hebrews to justify his methods, to prove that Melchizedek is Christ, but the writer of Hebrews was using the typological connection between the two *as* his proof. This means that he was operating in a different epistemological world than we do—and if we want to be faithful to the text, it is we who must learn how to change.

The tabernacle is another. Types and antitypes can function in history, bridging the Old and New Covenants, but they can also serve as a bridge between the Old Covenant and heaven. In the horizontal use, the type is in the Old Testament and the antitype is in the New. In the vertical use, the type is earthly *and early* and the antitype is heavenly. Sometimes it is the other way around (9:24). For an example of the former use, the law was a *shadow* of the good things to come (10:1). The whole temple apparatus was a *parable* for those using it (9:9). The whole served this function, and the details of the whole served this function (9:5). For an example of the vertical bridge, the earthly tabernacle and all its furniture were made according to the pattern shown to Moses on the mount. The tabernacle was a symbolic holy mountain and was built in accordance with the pattern that was shown to Moses *on* that holy mountain.

The emphasis in the New Testament leads us to draw a strong correlation between the heavenly things and New Covenant things—we who are in the New Covenant have a simpler form of worship than they did in the Old, and less typological, precisely because of our participation in the heavenly worship (12:22), and the free access we have been given to the heavenly courts (4:16).

A New Testament Deuteronomy

Seven Old Testament passages are quoted in the first chapter of Hebrews alone, and five of those seven passages have to do with the submission of the nations to Christ. That is the great subject of the book of Hebrews—and the author devotes himself to teaching us this. Almost forty explicit quotations from the Old Testament are here in this book, and this is not counting the numerous allusions and references. All of them fit into the story of the greater Joshua, subduing the nations of Canaan, that is, the nations of the world. When we look at how our author cites and applies Old Testament Scripture, if we are paying attention, we should be learning how to do this ourselves.

Think of the Old Testament as a large chart or map laid out on a table. Then roll the New Testament out over it, as an overlay. Then take a nail and drive it through both testaments, everywhere that the New Testament tells us what the Old Testament is talking about. Once those texts have been fixed, the rest of the Scriptures should be interpreted accordingly. This is commentary, but unlike the commentaries we come up with, it is *inspired* commentary. And one of the most astonishing things about our uninspired commentaries is how little we rely on the inspired commentary. When was the last time you were reading a commentary on Genesis and found the writer saying, "Of course, we recognize that the flood is emblematic of Christian baptism, as the apostle Peter tells us . . ." or, "These two women Sarah and Hagar represent two covenants, as Paul argues in Galatians"? To the extent that commentators recognize that the New Testament handling of these passages even exists, it is usually treated as a problem, and not as the *solution* it is. Take this passage for example: "For he has said, 'I will never leave you nor forsake you' "(Heb. 13:5b).

This text is what we might call a naturally inspirational one. "I will never leave you" is a text you might want to have imprinted on a cocoa mug for a rainy day, or on a Christian inspirational poster portraying a glorious California sunset. But a far better image for such a poster would be a panoramic view of Normandy beach just before the invasion. This is a quotation from Deuteronomy 31, and here is the original context:

> "The LORD your God himself will go over before you. He will destroy these nations before you, so that you shall dispossess

> them . . . And the LORD will give them over to you, and you shall do to them according to the whole commandment that I have commanded you. Be strong and courageous. Do not fear or be in dread of them, for it is the LORD your God who goes with you. He will not leave you or forsake you." (vv. 3–6)

It is also noteworthy that this promise from Deuteronomy is also quoted in the *next* book, Joshua, the book that describes the course of the invasion. Note the military language.

> "No man shall be able to stand before you all the days of your life. Just as I was with Moses, so I will be with you. *I will not leave you or forsake you.* Be strong and courageous, for you shall cause this people to inherit the land that I swore to their fathers to give them. Only be strong and very courageous, being careful to do according to all the law that Moses my servant commanded you. Do not turn from it to the right hand or to the left, that you may have good success wherever you go." (Josh. 1:5–7)

Moreover, especially when we see how Hebrews applies it to the establishment and building of the church, we should be struck by this same language when David is giving Solomon a charge to build the temple—the type of the church. "Then David said to Solomon his son, 'Be strong and courageous and do it. Do not be afraid and do not be dismayed, for the LORD God, even my God, is with you. *He will not leave you or forsake you*, until all the work for the service of the house of the LORD is finished' " (1 Chron. 28:20).

The book of Hebrews is a New Testament Deuteronomy. This can be seen in a number of ways. First, Hebrews quotes the book of Deuteronomy five times, three times from chapter 32. This is the chapter containing the Song of Moses, the great reminder of the entire book of Deuteronomy, the chapter that sums up all the issues. Second, the book of Hebrews places the recipients of this letter as an antitype for the people of Israel in the wilderness—at the end of which the book of Deuteronomy was given to them (Heb. 3: 7–4:11). Third, the people who first read the book of Hebrews were on the threshold of God's great invasion of the world, and this is how they were encouraged (Heb. 13:5; Deut. 31:6). Never will I leave you *during the course of the invasion of the land.*

And fourth, the structure of the book of Hebrews (generally) follows the same structure as that of Deuteronomy. There is a preamble (1–2), a historical prologue (3–4:15), general stipulations (4:16–7), specific stipulations (8–10), divine witnesses are called (11), and the book concludes with blessings and curses (12–13). As Craigie discusses the structure of Deuteronomy, we see similarities: there is a preamble (1:1–5), a historical prologue (1:6–4:49), general stipulations (5–11), specific stipulations (12–26), blessings and curses (27–28), and then the witnesses, just slightly out of place (30:19; 31:19; 32:1–43).[1] Some commentators make a great deal out of the fact that this pattern closely resembles the suzerain/vassal treaties of that era in the Middle East—but that is not my point here. My point is much simpler. It is striking that Deuteronomy and Hebrews are so structurally similar. Combine this with their common thematic elements, and the point becomes plain.

First, Hebrews invokes Deuteronomy and its themes. Second, Hebrews says that the Jews in the wilderness were a type of Christians in the wilderness. Third, the people of God in both instances were on the brink of an invasion and conquest. And last, the two books have the same general structure. We are supposed to be settled in this context (and *not* another one) when we read the book of Hebrews.

Immediately after Hebrews 13:5, the author of Hebrews quotes Psalm 118. This is the psalm that speaks of Christ (the stone the builders rejected, verses 22–23; and see 1 Peter 2:7; Acts 4:11; Luke 20:17; Mark 12:10–11; Matthew 21:42); and which also blessed the Christ who came in the name of the Lord (v. 26; Matt. 21:9; John 12:13; Mark 11:9; Luke 13:35; 19:38). This is the context of what the author of Hebrews quotes: "Out of my distress I called on the LORD; the LORD answered me and set me free. The LORD is on my side; I will not fear. What can man do to me? The LORD is on

---

1. Peter Craige, *The Book of Deuteronomy* (Grand Rapids, MI; Eerdmans, 1976), 24.

my side as my helper; I shall look in triumph on those who hate me" (Ps. 118:5–7).

The biblical faith, lived as it should be lived, will always generate resistance and conflict. This should not be a surprise; it should not come as a shock. The charge we are given in this context is the charge to be strong and courageous. This means that we are in the midst of circumstances where it would be easy *not* to be courageous, and *not* to be strong. What is God's role in this? He does the "not leaving." He does the "not forsaking." What do we do? We believe him when he says this, and the natural response to this faith is *courage*.

This means, then, that courage is a function of knowing two basic things about history. The first is knowing where you are in that history, and the second is knowing that God is with you during that particular moment of history. If you know where you are, but not where God is, that is despair. And if you know right where God is (in your heart), but you have no idea where *you* are, all you can do is maintain your devotional life until you die and go to heaven. But God is with you, and he is with us, and we are in the land of this world, an antitype of the land of Canaan. Where in the antitype history are we? We are somewhere in the book of Judges, slowly, surely—seeing both victories and reverses—subduing the land. And, no matter how grim it may look, God will never forsake us.

2

An Orientation to Hebrews

Before beginning our work in Hebrews verse by verse, we need to start with an "orientation." We already spoke of laying a New Testament transparency over a copy of the Old Testament and seeing how the New Testament uses the Old Testament in each instance. Since this is a commentary on the book of Hebrews, one of our first tasks should be to line up the Old Testament texts that are quoted in Hebrews. Before you begin a task, you calibrate your tools. Before going hunting, you sight in your rifle. Before studying a New Testament book, you look at its relationship to the Old Testament. You calibrate your instruments before you use them.

In the section that follows, you will find a sampling of quotations (or strong allusions) from the Old Testament in the book of Hebrews on the right, and the passage that is quoted (along with some context) is on the left. Beneath each pair I will make a few comments. A complete list of these quotations can be found in Appendix A.

The LORD says to my Lord: **Sit at my right hand**, until I make your enemies your footstool. (Ps. 110:1)

He is the radiance of the glory of God and the exact imprint of his nature, and he upholds the universe by the word of his power. After making purification for sins, he **sat down at the right hand** of the Majesty on high. (Heb. 1:3)

This psalm is frequently quoted in the New Testament. In it we find the kingship of Christ over all creation ("Sit at my right hand"), and at the end we also find that the Messiah is a priest after the order of Melchizedek, which is brought up later in Hebrews.

I will tell of the decree: The LORD said to me, "**You are my Son; today I have begotten you**. Ask of me, and I will make the nations your heritage, and the ends of the earth your possession." (Ps. 2:7–8)

For to which of the angels did God ever say, "**You are my Son, today I have begotten you**"? (Heb. 1:5a)

When we look at how Paul quotes Psalm 2 in Acts 13, we see that it is a reference to the resurrection. And in this psalm, immediately after the resurrection, God gives the Messiah all the Gentile nations for his inheritance.

And he said, "Hear my words: If there is a prophet among you, I the LORD make myself known to him in a vision; I speak with him in a dream. **Not so with my servant Moses. He is faithful in all my house**. With him I speak mouth to mouth, clearly, and not in riddles, and he beholds the form of the LORD. Why then were you not afraid to speak against my servant Moses?" And the anger of the LORD was kindled against them, and he departed. (Num. 12:6–9)

Therefore, holy brothers, you who share in a heavenly calling, consider Jesus, the apostle and high priest of our confession, who was faithful to him who appointed him, just as **Moses also was faithful in all God's house** . . . Now **Moses was faithful in all God's house** as a servant, to testify to the things that were to be spoken later. (Heb. 3:1–2, 5)

To describe Moses as a faithful servant in the house of God was not a demotion that the New Testament arranged for Moses. Moses understood himself this way.

And to Adam he said, "Because you have listened to the voice of your wife and have eaten of the tree of which I commanded you, 'You shall not eat of it,' **cursed is the ground** because of you; in pain you shall eat of it all the days of your life; **thorns and thistles it shall bring forth for you**; and you shall eat the plants of the field." (Gen. 3:17–18)

But if **it bears thorns and thistles**, it is worthless and **near to being cursed**, and its end is to be burned. (Heb. 6:8)

The earth was cursed as a result of the sin of the first man. In a similar way, when professing Christians refuse to hear the grace of salvation in faith, *their* ground has the same thing happen to it. The cursed ground of Genesis is a type of the unbelieving covenant member.

The LORD has sworn and will not change his mind, "**You are a priest forever after the order of Melchizedek.**" (Ps. 110:4)

. . . where Jesus has gone as a forerunner on our behalf, having become a high **priest forever after the order of Melchizedek** (Heb. 6:20).

This is yet another citation of Psalm 110. Christ is a priest in the same way that Melchizedek was a priest.

And see that you make them after the pattern for them, which is being shown you on the mountain. (Ex. 25:40)

They serve a copy and shadow of the heavenly things. For when Moses was about to erect the tent, he was instructed by God, saying, "**See that you make everything according to the pattern that was shown you on the mountain.**" (Heb. 8:5)

Moses was commanded to follow the divine blueprints in the building of the tabernacle. The tabernacle was a portable "mountain," and its structure followed the pattern that was shown to Moses on the mountain. That pattern in turn was taken from the heavenly tabernacle on the heavenly mountain, the ultimate mountain.

"**Behold, the days are coming, declares the LORD, when I will make a new covenant with the house of Israel and the house of Judah, not like the covenant that I made with their fathers on the day when I took them by the hand to bring them out of the land of Egypt, my covenant that they broke, though I was their husband, declares the LORD. But this is the covenant that I will make with the house of Israel after those days, declares the LORD: I will put my law within them, and I will write it on their hearts. And I will be their God, and they shall be my people. And no longer shall each one teach his neighbor and each his brother, saying, 'Know the LORD,' for they shall all know me, from the least of them to the greatest, declares the LORD. For I will forgive their iniquity, and I will remember their sin no more.**" (Jer. 31:31–34)

For he finds fault with them when he says: "**Behold, the days are coming, declares the Lord, when I will establish a new covenant with the house of Israel and with the house of Judah, not like the covenant that I made with their fathers on the day when I took them by the hand to bring them out of the land of Egypt. For they did not continue in my covenant, and so I showed no concern for them, declares the Lord. For this is the covenant that I will make with the house of Israel after those days, declares the Lord: I will put my laws into their minds, and write them on their hearts, and I will be their God, and they shall be my people. And they shall not teach, each one his neighbor and each one his brother, saying, 'Know the Lord,' for they shall all know me, from the least of them to the greatest. For I will be merciful toward their iniquities, and I will remember their sins no more.**" In speaking of a new covenant, he makes the first one obsolete. And what is becoming obsolete and growing old is ready to vanish away. (Heb. 8:8–13)

This great passage from Jeremiah is quoted twice in Hebrews. This is the first, with a full quotation. The intelligent reader of the

Old Testament for the first time would necessarily come away with the question "Where is the sequel?" The whole thing is longing for fulfillment, and this passage is one of the best examples of it. In the second quotation, in chapter 10, the passage is abridged, with the excerpts showing the most important features of the New Covenant—the internalization of the law, and the forgiveness of sins.

LORD, when thy hand is lifted up, they will not see: but they shall see, and be ashamed for their envy at the people; yea, **the fire of thine enemies shall devour them.** (Is. 26:11, LXX [Septuagint])	. . . but a fearful expectation of judgment, and a **fury of fire that will consume the adversaries**. (Heb. 10:27)

The writer of Hebrews frequently quotes the Septuagint, the translation of the Hebrew Old Testament into Greek. According to Jewish tradition, it was accomplished by seventy (LXX) scholars, hence the name, the Septuagint, or LXX.

This is actually a very important citation. One of the temptations that modern Christians have is that of assuming that any discussion of fire in the context of judgment must mean hellfire—eternal condemnation. But the context of Hebrews makes it clear that the potential apostates here are being warned against returning to Jerusalem, which was soon to be destroyed by the Roman armies. The fact that this kind of language is taken from Isaiah's rejoicing over the establishment of the New Covenant confirms this view.

" '**Vengeance is mine, and recompense**, for the time when their foot shall slip; for the day of their calamity is at hand, and their doom comes swiftly.' **For the LORD will vindicate his people** and have compassion on his servants, when he sees that their power is gone and there is none remaining, bond or free." (Deut. 32:35–36)	For we know him who said, "**Vengeance is mine; I will repay**." And again, "**The Lord will judge his people**." (Heb. 10:30)

God does not say that vengeance is wrong, but rather that "vengeance is mine." God (again, in both testaments) visits judgment *on his own people*. This does not refer to his elect, but it most certainly applies to his people in some sense.

But Sarah saw the son of Hagar the Egyptian, whom she had borne to Abraham, laughing. So she said to Abraham, "Cast out this slave woman with her son, for the son of this slave woman shall not be heir with my son Isaac." And the thing was very displeasing to Abraham on account of his son. But God said to Abraham, "Be not displeased because of the boy and because of your slave woman. Whatever Sarah says to you, do as she tells you, **for through Isaac shall your offspring be named**. And I will make a nation of the son of the slave woman also, because he is your offspring." (Gen. 21:9–13)

By faith Abraham, when he was tested, offered up Isaac, and he who had received the promises was in the act of offering up his only son, of whom it was said, "Through **Isaac shall your offspring be named**." (Heb. 11:17–18)

This is the hinge, this is the promise. And it meant that Isaac could not die (permanently) without having had children.

My son, do not despise the LORD's discipline or be weary of his reproof, for the LORD reproves him whom he loves, as a father the son in whom he delights. (Prov. 3:11–12)

And have you forgotten the exhortation that addresses you as sons? "**My son, do not regard lightly the discipline of the Lord, nor be weary when reproved by him. For the Lord disciplines the one he loves, and chastises every son whom he receives." It is for discipline that you have to endure. God is treating you as sons. For what son is there whom his father does not discipline**? (Heb. 12:5–7)

This quotation from Proverbs—a book from a father to his son—seeks to make a similar application to these first century Christians, who clearly were discouraged children.

And you came near and stood at the foot of the mountain, while the mountain burned with fire to the heart of heaven, wrapped in darkness, cloud, and gloom. Then the LORD spoke to you out of the midst of the fire. You heard the sound of words, but saw no form; there was only a voice. (Deut. 4:11–12)

For you have not come to what may be touched, a blazing fire and darkness and gloom and a tempest and the sound of a trumpet and a voice whose words made the hearers beg that no further messages be spoken to them. (Heb. 12:18–19)

There are many places in the book of Hebrews where parallels or heightened parallels between Old and New Testaments are drawn. But there are also places where contrasts are set before us. This is one of those places. The physical mountain of Sinai was shrouded in terrifying darkness—the New Covenant saints have *not* come to that kind of a mountain. But at the same time, the book of Hebrews teaches that there is a sense in which the New Covenant is *more* terrifying.

Be strong and courageous. Do not fear or be in dread of them, for it is the LORD your God who goes with you. He will not leave you or forsake you." Then Moses summoned Joshua and said to him in the sight of all Israel, "Be strong and courageous, for you shall go with this people into the land that the LORD has sworn to their fathers to give them, and you shall put them in possession of it. It is the LORD who goes before you. He will be with you; **he will not leave you or forsake you**. Do not fear or be dismayed." (Deut. 31:6–8)

Keep your life free from love of money, and be content with what you have, for he has said, "**I will never leave you nor forsake you**." (Heb. 13:5)

> No man shall be able to stand before you all the days of your life. Just as I was with Moses, so I will be with you. **I will not leave you or forsake you**. (Josh. 1:5)

"I will never leave you" sounds like a nice little inspirational quote. And it is, but not a quote to cheer us up on a rainy day. The people of Israel are on the brink of invasion, and God is promising to be with them in the thick of the fighting.

3

Key Texts

Now that we have looked at how the book of Hebrews handles the Old Testament generally, we can do a little additional spadework as we prepare ourselves to study this epistle. Nothing is more apparent than that the writer of this letter was marinated in Scripture. As Spurgeon said of Bunyan, prick him anywhere and his blood would run bibline. Even more so, the author of Hebrews would bleed Bible verses.

When we look at how the entire New Testament handles the Old Testament, one of the things we learn is which books the New Testament writers quote most frequently. There are four—Genesis, Deuteronomy, Psalms, and Isaiah. In a sense, we may say that these four books are New Testament "favorites." Because we have the most help from the New Testament writers on these four books, this means that we can make the most efficient use of our time. If we are novices in the Old Testament Scriptures—as the writer and recipients of this letter were *not*—then we have to do some preparatory work in the Old Testament to be able even to join the conversation. Far too many "New Testament" Christians think that the New Testament is a course that has no prerequisites, when in fact, jumping into New Testament studies without Old Testament grounding is like going straight from kindergarten to graduate physics. Either the student will be overwhelmed, or he will be extraordinarily diligent and hardworking, making sense out of it for himself, but with the result being an exotic creation of his own.

If we begin by looking carefully at some of the key texts that the author of Hebrews deals with extensively, we will fare much better. Those texts are Deuteronomy 31–32, Psalm 2, Psalm 8, Psalm 22, Psalm 40, Psalm 95, Psalm 110, and Jeremiah 31.

DEUTERONOMY 31–32

Although Israel will ultimately fail in her invasion of Canaan, the second Israel will never fail in her invasion of the world. Although the ancient people of God were corrupted by idolatry, the people of God today cannot ultimately fall in the same way. Jesus Christ is victor. *"So Moses continued to speak these words to all Israel. . . ."* (Deut. 31:1–30).

The book of Deuteronomy is coming to a close, and the time has come for Moses to die. God promises them that they will enjoy great victory as they cross over into the land (vv. 1–6). God will go before them, but in his kindness he will not leave them without human leadership (vv. 7–8). Moses wrote down the law, and commanded that it be read to Israel every seven years (vv. 9–13). Joshua is summoned and God sets him apart as the replacement of Moses (vv. 14–15, 23). God then predicts that the people will in fact turn away after Moses' death (vv. 16–18). Moses writes his song, and teaches it to Israel (vv. 19–23). After this, Moses delivers the law as an additional testimony against them (vv. 24–30).

But first there is initial victory. Moses is one hundred and twenty years old (vv. 1–2) and can no longer lead the people. God will lead them over Jordan, and Joshua will lead them also (v. 3). The Canaanites will perish like Og and Sihon (v. 4). God will give them victory so that they might obey in that victory (v. 5), and therefore Israel is summoned to strength and courage (v. 6).

Moses calls Joshua and encourages him (v. 7). God will go with Joshua and will not forsake him (v. 8). There is no reason for discouragement or dismay. They have been given the liberty of covenant law. Moses wrote down the law and delivered it to the priests (v. 9). Moses commanded the reading of the law every seven years (v. 10), in the year of release. The law was to be read in the hearing of all—men, women, children, and aliens (vv. 11–12). The law was to be read particularly for the children (v. 13). They would hear it read once (and perhaps twice) in their childhood.

We return to the commissioning of Joshua, the type of Jesus, the replacement of Moses. God warned Moses that he was to die soon (v. 14). God had both men stand before the congregation so that Joshua could be charged. The Lord then appeared in the pillar of cloud at the door of the tabernacle (v. 15).

The subject then turns to the coming apostasy. Joshua is to be encouraged, but not because the people will be permanently faithful. The people will break the covenant (v. 16). God will forsake them in anger, and they will realize the cause of their desolation (v. 17), and God will hide his face from them because of their idolatry (v. 18).

We then have a testimony to the power of liturgy. God tells Moses to write and teach a song as a testimony (v. 19). They will grow fat and turn away (v. 20). In their tribulation, the song will witness against them (v. 21). The root of their apostasy was present even before they entered the land (v. 21). Moses writes and teaches the song (v. 22), and he delivers a solemn charge to Joshua (v. 23).

So Moses finally finishes writing (v. 24). He then commands the Levites to put it in the side of the ark as a witness against them (vv. 25–26). They have been rebellious; they will be rebellious again (v. 27). He then summons all the elders and officers so that he might warn them (v. 28), for he knows they will fall (v. 29), and then Moses speaks the words of the song (v. 30).

The only way to be encouraged in *this* world is through faith.

The law is your life—do you see the law of God (*rightly*, by grace) as the release from debt? Or the incurring of it? *Be strong and courageous*—the same exhortation applies to us today in the conquest of the world (Heb. 13:5). This is the place where the writer to the Hebrews brings the book of Deuteronomy to bear.

We have been anticipating this song, but the time has now come to learn it. The theme of the song echoes many of the themes of the entire book of Deuteronomy: "*Give ear, O heavens, and I will speak, and let the earth hear the words of my mouth. . . .*" (Deut. 32:1–52).

The song begins and the witnesses of heaven and earth are summoned (vv. 1–6). Verses 7–14 contain a historical review and the speech of the prosecutor. The specific charge against Israel is found next (vv. 15–18). God as the judge then pronounces the sentence (vv. 19–26), and a lamentation follows (vv. 27–33). In verse 34, the judge deliberates. The decision following that deliberation is next (vv. 35–42) and the concluding doxology is found in verse 43. When the song is concluded, Moses gives a final exhoration (vv. 44–47). God then commands Moses to climb the mountain where he will die (vv. 48–52).

This is doctrinal rain. Heavens and earth are called as witnesses (v. 1). The teaching of the song will fall like soft, life-giving rain (v. 2). The point is to ascribe greatness to God (v. 3), who is a Rock without iniquity (v. 4). The people are notably unlike him in this (v. 5). Is this how you pay him back, O Israel (v. 6)? Is this how you repay your father? Remember the days of old, consider the years (v. 7). God divided the sons of Adam in accordance with the number of the sons of God (v. 8, LXX). But Israel was not like the others; they were *God's* portion (v. 9). As Israel's God, he took them under his protection (vv. 10–11). God led them, there were no other gods (v. 12). And the Lord God blessed Israel enormously (vv. 13–14).

But Jeshurun (v. 15) grew fat and kicked. Blessings are intended to bring gratitude, but they frequently bring insolence. What is the nature of the provocation? Always idolatry (v. 16). The demonic nature of idolatry is plainly stated (v. 17). In short, they forgot their God who formed them (v. 18).

So judgment falls. God abhorred his sons and daughters and their provocations (v. 19). He turned his face away to see what would become of those without faith (v. 20). I am their God and they are my people; if they insist on provoking me to jealousy with their worship of no-God, then I will provoke them to jealousy with my salvation of no-people (v. 21). Judgments will follow and fall—fire, arrows, famine, heat, wild animals, the poison of serpents—and none will be spared (vv. 22–25).

God himself does not want their enemies to gloat (vv. 26–27). They are a vacant nation, a hollow people (v. 28). O, that they were wise! (v. 29). They could not be defeated unless God had sold them (v. 30). The nation defeating them has no rock (v. 31), and they are a corrupt people (v. 32). Their poison is that of dragons (v. 33), that is, deceitful.

It belongs to God alone to act (v. 34). Their foot shall slide in due time (v. 35). God will judge his people (v. 36). The Lord himself will taunt them for the impotence of their idols (vv. 37–38). God will judge, and none can hold him back (vv. 39–42). The Gentiles are called to rejoice in that judgment (v. 43).

Moses ends the song (vv. 44–45). His last exhortation is for them to set their hearts to the law (v. 46). It is not a vain thing; how could their life be a vain thing (v. 47)? God tells him to climb (vv. 48–49) and die (v. 50). Moses could not enter because of his sin at Meribah-Kadesh (v. 51), but he was allowed to see the land where he would one day stand with Jesus and Elijah (v. 52).

Again, we look to the New Testament for understanding. *We are the no-people*—this song remains a prophetic word (verse 21 and Romans 10:19). Note verse 43 and Romans 15:10. *Vengeance is mine*—verses 35 and 36 are quoted in Hebrews 10:30. Verse 35 is quoted in Romans 12:19. This means the standards of covenantal faithfulness so clearly set forth here are standards that remain in place—the author of Hebrews uses them, and plainly applies them.

PSALM 2

In this psalm we have a wonderful prophecy of the reign of Messiah the Prince. The prophecy does *not* concern the reign of God in his sovereignty, which is the necessary result of the Creator's relationship with the world he created, but rather a reign that *results* from his sovereign decree—the mediatorial reign of the Lord Jesus Christ. In other words, God has always ruled the world. But he rules the world *redemptively* through Jesus Christ. "*Why do the nations rage, and the people peoples plot in vain . . . ?*" (Ps. 2:1–12).

We are *Christians*, and this means, among other things, that we should seek to have the New Testament teach us what the Old Testament means. Our method for learning the meaning of this psalm is to pay close attention to what the New Testament says about it. These New Testament references should always be our anchor points.

Why do the nations rage? We are told in Acts 4:24–28 that the first two verses of the second psalm are a prophecy of the *crucifixion*. We also learn of the Davidic authorship of the psalm there. In addition, we see that the psalm is the basis for saying that the murder of Christ was predestined. God used the wickedness of men to save the world.

Now in Acts 13:33, we learn that verse 7 of this psalm is a prophecy of the *resurrection*. This verse is quoted in two other places also. Hebrews 1:5 shows us that this passage requires the supremacy of Christ over angels. Hebrews 5:5 quotes it as describing Christ entering his office as high priest. Put them all together, and we see that in the resurrection, Christ is begotten from the dead, enters into his high priestly work, and is made higher than the angels.

Then there is the rod of iron. The book of Revelation refers to verse 9 three times, and the usage there is very interesting. Revelation 19:15–16 refers to Christ's rule over the nations, with his wrath in view. Revelation 12:5 refers simply to Christ's rule over the nations. And Revelation 2:26–29 teaches us that Christ rules the nations *through his saints*. God has made us kings and priests on the earth.

So what are the implications of this? This psalm has twelve verses. We now know that verses 1 and 2 are about the crucifixion, that verse 7 is about the resurrection, and that verse 9 addresses the reign of Christ through his Word in the church. What then do we learn from the rest of the psalm? Having established fixed points in the psalm (fixed by authoritative commentary from the New Testament), we are in a position to see what the rest of it means. The language of verse 3 refers to the nations' resentment over the fact that they had to plow underneath the yoke of the Lord Jesus Christ.

Then we come to the laughter of God. Consider two things. First, if the laughter of God can accomplish such great and terrible things, what will his wrath be like? And secondly, who would have thought of this—divine *laughter*—when the sun was dark, the disciples scattered, our Lord in anguish, the Sanhedrin gloating, Satan triumphant, Peter wretched, Judas in despair, and Mary in tears? Yet God will do what he has intended to do through all this. Despite their pitiful little schemes, the Lord will establish his king in Zion (v. 6), however little they like it (v. 5).

Now after the crucifixion, and just after the resurrection, God Almighty extends an invitation to his Son, Jesus Christ—he invites him to *just ask* (v. 8). What belongs to Jesus Christ now? What nation is not his present possession? Can you find *one*? Is there one he *didn't* want? Did he refuse to ask for one? Remember, the rod of iron extends over them all (v. 9).

What therefore is the responsibility of our Congress, our Supreme Court, and our president? They must seek wisdom and receive instruction. They must serve God in their public *civic* capacity, with fear, joy, and trembling (v. 11). Remember that God's laughter overthrew all their impudent plans. Beware of his wrath (v.12). This means that the United States, or Great Britain, or whatever other nation this may be, has the explicit duty to be a Christian nation.

When the church hears the Word of God rightly, the whole world is set to rights. The three great offices of Christ are set before us in this psalm. He is the prophet—we must hear his words of instruction (v. 10). He is king, established in Zion (v. 6), and he is priest (v. 7; Heb. 5:5). We see that the Lord has already received his inheritance. The matter is settled. The question is not being brought before the United Nations for consideration. The reign of Christ has been established. The nations who object to this settlement trouble the decrees of God about as much as dogs barking at the moon trouble the moon.

This is why Jesus Christ reigns redemptively throughout the entire earth. Christians are those who are called to believe what God has declared concerning this. The one who trusts his Word is always blessed. God has spoken on this glorious subject—are we blessed in hearing it? Do we believe him? Jesus reigns from the river to the ends of the earth. Which river? It does not matter. From the Thames to the Hudson, from the Nile to the Ganges, from the Rhine to the Mississippi, from the Potomac to the Amazon, the name of the Lord will be praised, and pure sacrifices will be offered up to him in every nation.

PSALM 8

The eighth psalm is another psalm of David. The import of the psalm is glorious and joyful. "*O LORD, our Lord, how majestic is your name in all the earth! You have set your glory above the heavens. . . .*" (Ps. 8:1–9).

We see first how the creation gives glory to God. The details of this psalm are sandwiched between two examples of high exultation (vv. 1, 9). God's name is excellent in all the earth, and his glory is above the heavens. We should then note victory out of the mouths of babes. Those who hate God and resist his will are defeated by him. God defeats them in the words of *babies* (v. 2). Who shuts down the railing atheist? The answer of this psalm is the jabbering baby in the back of the sanctuary. *He* is the one who silences the foe and the avenger.

Of course this relates to humility. When a man with a right heart considers the work of God's fingers in the heavens, he is abased and overwhelmed. Part of this is because God continues his kindnesses on our tiny level (vv. 3–4). But despite a humble man's awareness that he is merely a piece of clay, God has nevertheless placed him just beneath in the angels in rank (v. 5), and has crowned him with glory and honor. The Lord Jesus came and occupied this place that was a little lower than the angels, and in so doing, he exalted that place forever. We therefore see true dominion: man is steward of the earth, and God has made him vicegerent over all beasts, birds, and fish (vv. 6–8).

We should carefully note the anchor points of this psalm. This psalm is frequently quoted in the New Testament, just as Psalm 2 was, and we must use these quotations as anchor points in our interpretation of it. If we do not, then we will miss the point of the psalm entirely. One of the great tragedies in biblical commentary is how *infrequently* believing Christians take at face value the authoritative words of the New Testament on what an Old Testament passage means.

We have already commented on one of these places—"out of the mouths of babes." Jesus quotes the second verse of this psalm when certain self-important theologians were distressed over the behavior of children at Christ's triumphal entry into Jerusalem (Matt. 21:15–16). There is also a possible allusion to this psalm in Matthew 11:25. God has hidden these things from the wise and prudent, and revealed them to *babes*. And to this day, theologians continue to shoo babies away from Jesus.

And all things have been placed "under his feet." Whose feet? In the book of Hebrews, the apostle Paul applies this psalm *to mankind in Christ*.

> Now it was not to angels that God subjected the world to come, of which we are speaking. It has been testified somewhere,
>
> "What is man, that you are mindful of him,
> or the son of man, that you care for him?
> You made him for a little while lower than the angels;
> you have crowned him with glory and honor,
> putting everything in subjection under his feet."
>
> Now in putting everything in subjection to him, he left nothing outside his control. At present, we do not yet see everything in subjection to him. But we see him who for a little while was made

> lower than the angels, namely Jesus, crowned with glory and honor because of the suffering of death, so that by the grace of God he might taste death for everyone. (Heb. 2:5–9)

We see the same thing in 1 Corinthians. Here Paul applies the psalm *to Christ*. "For he must reign until he has put all his enemies under his feet. The last enemy to be destroyed is death. For 'God has put all things in subjection under his feet.' But when it says, 'all things are put in subjection,' it is plain that he is excepted who put all things in subjection under him. When all things are subjected to him, then the Son himself will also be subjected to him who put all things in subjection under him, that God may be all in all" (1 Cor. 15:25–28).

Paul emphasizes this theme in Ephesians also. In Christ, mankind comes into his dominion. "That he worked in Christ when he raised him from the dead and seated him at his right hand in the heavenly places, far above all rule and authority and power and dominion, and above every name that is named, not only in this age but also in the one to come. And he put *all things under his feet* and gave him as head over all things *to the church*, which is his body, the fullness of him who fills all in all" (Eph. 1:20–23).

Mankind is in the process of growing up to his maturity in Christ. But in recent times, our difficulty in understanding covenantal identity has really crippled us. Jesus Christ is not the *isolated* perfect man. Jesus Christ is the new mankind, he is the new Adam, he is the new race of man. And all who are in him are included in this glorious new dominion.

The ruin created by the first Adam is being repaired in the person and work of the second Adam. We are invited to see the restoration of the entire earth in Christ—and if we are more dependent on our newspapers than on the Word of God, the author of Hebrews both encourages and admonishes us. We do not *yet* see everything subject to mankind in Christ, but we *do* see Jesus Christ, and to the extent we see him by faith, in line with what the New Testament teaches about this, the world will be subdued under the preaching of the gospel.

Everything has been placed under the feet of Jesus Christ. But we are his body; *we* are his feet.

PSALM 22

This psalm contains one of the great Old Testament portrayals of the gospel. Along with Isaiah 53, we learn here that the death of Christ for the sins of the world was no afterthought. The Lamb of God was indeed slain from before the foundations of the world. *"My God, my God, why have you forsaken me? Why are you so far from saving me, from the words of my groaning? O my God, I cry by day, but you do not answer, and by night, but I find no rest. . . ."* (Psalm 22:1–31).

Christ cries out, forsaken by his Father (v. 1). He receives no answer (v. 2), and yet he knows that God, the one who inhabits Israel's praises, is holy (v. 3). Our fathers cried out to God, and *they* were heard (vv. 4–5). But the Lord, at least for the present, is in a different place; they despise him (vv. 6–7) and they taunt him for his faith (v. 8). The response of the Lord Jesus is to remind himself of his life-long faith in God (vv. 9–10), and he then renews his request for God to deliver (v. 11, 19). Between these two verses, we see how desperate his circumstances were: he was surrounded by threatening bulls (vv. 12–13); he was poured out like water and his bones were out of joint (v. 14); his heart was like wax (v. 14); his strength was dried like a potsherd, and he was brought down to the dust of death (v. 15); dogs have surrounded him, and his hands and feet were pierced (v. 16); he could count his bones (v. 17); and gamblers competed for his clothing (v. 18). His cry for deliverance resumed—he cried out to be saved from the lion and the unicorn (vv. 20–21).

After his great despairing cry *of faith*, the second half of the psalm is the triumphant cry of faith. He will praise God in the congregation (v. 22). All who fear God are summoned to join in the praise (v. 23). Why is this? God answers the prayer of the faithful, *including this one* (v. 24). Christ shall praise God in the great congregation (v. 25). The meek (who will inherit the earth) shall also eat and be satisfied (v. 26). All the ends of the earth shall be converted and turn to the Lord, and they will worship him (v. 27). The Lord has conquered the world through his faithful despairing (v. 28). Rich and poor alike shall serve him (v. 29), and the Lord shall have a seed (v. 30). They will testify that the Lord has done this (v. 31).

An ancient Christian tradition held that Christ on the cross began quoting Psalm 22 here, and he did not stop quoting the Psalter until he came to Psalm 31:5—"into your hand I commit my Spirit." Although we cannot assert this dogmatically, this certainly accords with what is happening. That moment on the cross is the fulfillment of *all* God's purposes, expressed so clearly throughout the entire Old Testament, and most particularly here. A man would have to be blind (and sadly many are) not to see how all these ancient words are coming to a glorious fruition.

Here is the certainty of God's Word. The words of this psalm were written about a thousand years before Christ. That is, chronologically David was to Christ what William the Conqueror is to us. One thousand years before it all happened, David saw, through the Spirit, that Christ's hands and feet were to be pierced (v. 16), that he would die at the hands of his enemies (vv. 12–13, 16), that his clothing would be gambled for (v. 18), and that he would die in agony (vv. 15, 17). For those of us who stumble in our faith, we are told that all of these things, taken together, will conquer the world (v. 27). Further, all these details of Christ's death were itemized in prophecy, and wicked men *blindly fulfilled all of it*, thinking themselves to be lords of the earth (1 Cor. 2:8; John 12: 32).

We therefore see the impotence of malice. There are many apparent reasons to take malice seriously. They are described here as raging (very powerful) bulls. They gape with their mouths in a terrifying way. The dogs are set loose, and the image is that of a hunted animal, like a stag, at bay. Ravening dogs surround the Lord's victim, but they do more than threaten. The Lord falls into their hands—*everything* is going their way. They mock him, but they also pierce him. They win, and they taunt as though they have won. They have the power of bulls, of ravening dogs, of a rampaging lion, of a vaunting unicorn. They exult as they hang the Messiah of God upon a gibbet, and lift him up . . . and accomplish the salvation of the entire world. Their murdering malice was the instrument of my salvation, and yours, and not ours only, but also the salvation of all the ends of the earth.

This is the heart of the gospel. We here see Christ forsaken by the Father. This is not to say that the Trinity unraveled, but rather that the unbroken fellowship between God and his incarnate Son is affected at this moment. This is not a cry of despairing faith, but rather a cry of faithful despair. When Christ experiences this abandonment by the Father, he quotes Scripture: it is still "*My* God, *my* God," and the psalm moves on to express that Christ on the cross had the glorious postmillennial vision right in front of him. The ends of the earth *will* turn, and the joy set before him was glorious (Heb. 12:2). The Lord knew that joy was set before him, as Hebrews says, because this psalm that began in despair ended in triumph.

What is it that accomplishes this? "For our sake he made him to be sin who knew no sin, so that in him we might become the righteousness of God" (2 Cor. 5:21). On the cross, Christ's despairing faith threw down all despair, sin, rebellion, and wickedness. *Christus victor*.

PSALM 40

While all the psalms are messianic, this fortieth psalm is a great and glorious messianic psalm. The New Testament plainly declares it to have been fulfilled in Christ, and, given this, we learn a great deal about what Jesus came to accomplish. "*I waited patiently for the Lord; he inclined to me, and heard my cry. . . .*" (Ps. 40:1–17).

There are three sections in this psalm. The first is a rejoicing testimony to the delivering power of God's goodness (vv. 1–3). The second is a meditation on the present goodness of God (vv. 4–10). The third is a prayer for deliverance in the future (vv. 11–17). God has been good in the past, he is good now, and the psalmist turns to him for salvation in the future. The New Testament fixes this psalm for us as an explicitly messianic psalm through how it is quoted and applied in Hebrews:

> Consequently, when Christ came into the world, he said,
> "Sacrifices and offerings you have not desired,
> but a body have you prepared for me;
> in burnt offerings and sin offerings
> you have taken no pleasure.
> Then I said, 'Behold, I have come to do your will, O God,
> as it is written of me in the scroll of the book.' "
>
> When he said above, "You have neither desired nor taken pleasure in sacrifices and offerings and burnt offerings and sin offerings" (these are offered according to the law), then he added, "Behold, I have come to do your will." He does away with the first in order to establish the second. And by that will we have been sanctified through the offering of the body of Jesus Christ once for all. (Heb. 10:5–10)

Before proceeding further, we need to clear up one trouble. In the Hebrew text of Psalm 40, verse 6 reads, "my ears you opened." This could be rendered as "my ears you have pierced," which appears to reflect the law in Exodus 21:6. "Then his master shall bring him to God, and he shall bring him to the door or the doorpost. And his master shall bore his ear through with an awl, and he shall be his slave forever."

However, the Septuagint (the Greek translation of the Old Testament, which is the version quoted in Hebrews) renders this as a "body have you prepared for me." This is most likely an *idiomatic* rendering of the Hebrew—the piercing of the ear meant total "consecration," and a body prepared by God amounts to the same thing. This is a figure of speech called synecdoche, where the whole is spoken of in terms of the part (e.g., "all hands on deck"). A pieced ear is the part representing the whole, a body fully dedicated to the service of God. There have been some other explanations, some of them quite ingenious, but this appears to be the simplest explanation.

The fact that this psalm is clearly about the Messiah does not mean that it is *not* about David. But the meaning of the psalm would vary according to how we were reading it. The messianic meaning does not displace the Davidic meaning. We can see the need for such distinctions clearly in verse 12, where he says "my iniquities have overtaken me." We read this differently, depending upon whether we are talking about David or David's great Son. But more about this shortly. When sinful men typify the sinless Christ, there must be adjustments in understanding made, but they must not be adjustments that simply set the point aside. We see this with Adam, with Joseph, with David, with Solomon, and so on.

The deliverance from the pit was preceded with *patience* (v. 1). Again, godly patience is not stoicism. "In the days of his flesh, Jesus offered up prayers and supplications, *with loud cries and tears*, to him who was able to save him from death, and he was heard because of his reverence" (Heb. 5:7). God delivered Jesus from a horrible pit, set him on a rock and established his goings (v. 2). Hades would certainly qualify as the ultimate of horrible pits, and God did not abandon Christ there. Having raised him from the dead, God placed a new song in the mouth of Christ, even praise to God. The result is that many will see it, and will trust in the Lord. *Christ's faith is the model for our faith.*

Blessed is the man who trusts God, and not the proud or those who veer off after lies (v. 4). We cannot count all the wonderful works that God has done for us (v. 5). There is no way to reckon the kindness of God. God did not desire mere conformity to ritual; he also wanted true obedience (v. 6). More about this in a moment. The Christ came to fulfill what was written in the book (v. 7). When he came, coming to earth to *die*, he said, "I *delight* to do your will" (v. 8). Christ, the one who came, was and is a great preacher (v. 9), and he was a preacher of *righteousness*. Do not reduce this to "a preacher of *morality*." We can see this in that he did not hide righteousness away, but rather declared God's faithfulness and salvation (v. 10). Righteousness is equated to faithfulness and *salvation*. As a preacher, Christ did not conceal God's loving-kindness or truth from the great congregation.

The assignment of a proper place to sacrifices is *not* a New Testament novelty at all. "And Samuel said, 'Has the LORD as great delight in burnt offerings and sacrifices, as in obeying the voice of the LORD? Behold, to obey is better than sacrifice, and to listen than the fat of rams' " (1 Sam. 15:22). "Hear the word of the LORD, 'What to me is the multitude of your sacrifices? says the LORD. . . . ' " (Is. 1:10–17; cf. Jer. 7:21–26). "For I desire steadfast love and not sacrifice, the knowledge of God rather than burnt offerings" (Hos. 6:6; cf. Micah 6:6–8).

Because God is faithful, there is shame for those who taunt. Let your loving-kindness preserve me forever (v. 11). Another wave of evils has surrounded the psalmist (v. 12), and his iniquities have seized him. They are more than the hairs of his head (v. 12). "God, hurry *up*" (v. 13). Defeat those who come against him (v. 14). Let those who taunt be shamed (v. 15; cf. 35:21; 70:3). Let all those who love God's salvation praise the Lord constantly (v. 16). The psalmist is poor and needy, and he asks God not to tarry (v. 17).

Christ never sinned. So how are we to understand the reference in verse 12 to iniquities? ("For evils have encompassed me beyond number; my iniquities have overtaken me, and I cannot see; they are more than the hairs of my head; my heart fails me.") Obviously, as it applies to David, we take it the same way we have taken it in other instances. But in this passage, is there a way to apply it to Christ also? *Yes*. "For our sake he made him *to be* sin who knew no sin, so that in him we might become the righteousness of God" (2 Cor. 5:21). Jesus Christ became a curse for us while hanging on the cross. The one who was never a sinner became (through God's imputation) completely identified with sin, *our* sin. He was completely identified with an innumerable host of sins, took them all upon himself, closed his arms upon them in an obedient embrace, and died. *That* is why there is no condemnation.

PSALM 95

This psalm begins with a joyful invitation, but ends with a grim warning. "O come, let us sing to the LORD: let us make a joyful noise to the rock of our salvation" (Ps. 95:1–11). In many ways this psalm is like a minister including careful warnings about the sin of divorce in his homily at a wedding ceremony. A wedding is a joyful occasion, and yet we live in a sinful world, and vows are included in the ceremony for a reason. In a similar way, the people of Israel were exuberant in their deliverance from the power of Egypt, and there was nothing wrong with their celebration beside the sea. The horse and rider were thrown into the sea, and it was right for Miriam and the women of Israel to sing. Yet when the celebration for that deliverance was over, they all had to turn and face the wilderness, and had to learn how to trust God in that wilderness. It was easier to sing about than to do.

All the people were invited to sing to God (v. 1) and to make a joyful noise to the rock of their salvation (v. 1). Gratitude and thanksgiving were to be brought before him, along with the joyful noise of psalms (v. 2). The reason for praising him was that he was a great God, not like the others; he was a great king over all the gods of all the other nations (v. 3). In the first place, he is the creator God—his hand holds all the treasures of the deep places of the earth, and he possesses the strength of the mountains and hills as well (v. 4). The ocean is his because he created it, and God's hands formed the dry land (v. 5).

Because God is the creator God, we should bow down and worship him as the one who made us (v. 6). Not only is he our maker, but he is also our shepherd. He is the creator God, and he is also the shepherd God (v. 7). Because God has bestowed all this care upon his people, they should take care *to listen to him*. And this brings us to the second part of the psalm, the portion repeatedly quoted in Hebrews.

Sing to God, for he is worthy of it. He is greater than all the idols. He is the maker of all things, and in his covenant care, he shepherds his people. This is the basis of the severe exhortation to follow, the one quoted in Hebrews 3:7–11, 3:15, 4:3, 4, and 4:7.

The first thing we must take from this into our reading of Hebrews is the joy and exuberance of the first portion of the psalm. The prospect of covenant curses does not unsettle the elect. We who have believed enter that rest, and the warnings only serve to establish us. But we must seek to be *established* in the warnings, and this will not happen so long as we are pretending that they are somehow inconsistent with our Calvinism. The warnings should be embraced and honored, not treated as a doctrinal problem.

In Hebrews 3:7–11, this entire section is quoted, introducing it to the argument in that epistle. In verse 15 of that same chapter the preamble of that passage is quoted again, "Today, if you hear his voice, do not harden your hearts." In Hebrews 4:3 and 5, the stark conclusion is quoted—"As I swore in my wrath . . ." And then in Hebrews 4:7, the beginning of the passage is cited again.

The whole point of doing this *was to draw a parallel* between the Jews in the wilderness and the Christian Jews in their "wilderness." The sins that the ancient Jews had committed were the same sins the first-century Christians were capable of committing. The opportunity of rest that had been set before them was also set before the first recipients of this letter. As we shall see in our discussion of Jeremiah, God had ensured the long-term success of his New Covenant people, but this promise for the people at large did not change the covenant dynamics for the individual believer. For the individual believer, apostasy was still a terrible thing.

The facile objection that this overturns the sovereignty of God's election of individuals is hardly worth a response. Of course God's sovereign election stands firm in the New Covenant, just as it did in the Old. The fact that God determined beforehand which Jews were going to remain faithful to him and which were not did not alter in the slightest the fact that the warnings were still directed at all his covenanted people, which included those who were going to fall. Not all Israel were of Israel.

In the same way, we have to take this grim warning in this psalm as a warning directed at baptized Christians. At the level of decretal theology, we must say that God will not judge his people because all the severities of his judgment were satisfied in the death of Christ. There is no possible condemnation for the elect. But at the level of the historical covenant, we must say (on equally scriptural grounds) that God will judge *his people*. And we must say that the book of Hebrews is filled with precisely this kind of warning.

PSALM 110

Psalm 110 is heavily quoted in the New Testament. The first verse ("The LORD says to my Lord . . .") is found in all three synoptic gospels, in Matthew 22:44, Mark 12:36, and Luke 20:42–43. The point of those citations is Christ's great question of the Jewish leaders: How can the Messiah be a descendant of David, a Davidson, and at the same time be a person David acknowledges as someone much greater? How could the great David call a descendant of his *Lord*? This question was actually quite a stumper. "And no man was able to answer him a word" (Matt. 22:46). "And the common people heard him gladly" (Mark 12:37).

The first verse is also quoted by Peter in his great Pentecostal sermon (Acts 2:34–35). Peter is proclaiming to all Israel that Jesus has been raised from the dead, and that moreover he has been enthroned at the right hand of God the Father.

> This Jesus God raised up, and of that we all are witnesses. Being therefore exalted at the right hand of God, and having received from the Father the promise of the Holy Spirit, he has poured out this that you yourselves are seeing and hearing. For David did not ascend into the heavens, but he himself says,
>
> " 'The Lord said to my Lord,
> Sit at my right hand,
> until I make your enemies your footstool.'
>
> Let all the house of Israel therefore know for certain that God has made him both Lord and Christ, this Jesus whom you crucified." (Acts 2:32–36)

Jesus had been raised from the dead, as the disciples witnessed. They saw him raised, but did not see him rising. They did see the moment when he ascended into the heavens (Acts 1:9), and they knew that God had fulfilled his promise to Christ by enthroning him there, and giving him the Holy Spirit, which Jesus then poured out at Pentecost. This was the explanation, Peter said, for all the marvels which you see around you.

The first verse of this very important psalm is quoted in the first chapter of Hebrews, and to the same effect. Christ has been given the pre-eminence that at the name of Jesus every knee should bow, whether in heaven, on earth, or under the earth. This being the case, and being so clear, we need to be wary of any interpretation of these words which does not grant all authority in heaven and on earth to Jesus Christ. The statement that God has given all things to Christ surely cannot be taken to mean that he has not given all things to Christ.

The Lord himself will extend the scepter of the Lord from Zion (v. 2), and he will then rule in the midst of his enemies. We know now that this Zion must be the heavenly Zion, the New Jerusalem, the Christian church. Christ is seated at the right hand of God, and believers are seated there with him. This is why we are kings and priests on the earth.

Because of who Christ is, and because of how he has been honored, his troops are more than willing for the battle of proclaiming the gospel (v. 3). The church is arrayed in majesty and glory, and will appear everywhere, like the dew on the ground in the morning.

Then we come to the fourth verse of this psalm, a verse that is quoted three times in the book of Hebrews (5:6, 7:17, and 7:21), and serves as a hinge for the argument. While the imagery of the first verse is regal, the image here is priestly. This means that Christ is going to be Joshua and Zerubabel together—he is going to be a priest/king, just like Melchizedek was.

The rule that Christ will extend over the earth will not come quietly. Kings will have to be crushed (v. 5). Nations will be judged, and there will be heaps of the dead. All over the earth, rulers of the earth will be crushed (v. 6). And in the aftermath of the battle, the king will drink from a brook by the way, and will lift up his head (v. 7). It is interesting that the psalm begins with the Lord Jesus at the right hand of the Father (v. 1), and concludes with the Lord Jesus at *David's* right hand, crushing all opposition. This is a type—Christ rules from the right hand of the Father, and because he has poured out the Holy Spirit (as Peter interpreted this psalm), he is present at *our* right hand as the message of the gospel goes out into the earth.

JEREMIAH 31

Jeremiah's great prophecy of the New Covenant comes from a section of his book that is rich with references to the time of Christ. Early in the chapter (31:15) is the prophecy quoted by Matthew (2:18) referring to the slaughter of the young boys by Herod. The prophecy of the New Covenant comes in verses 31 through 34. In the next chapter, Jeremiah buys a field as an acted-out prophecy—thus showing that despite the Babylonian siege, a time would come when land purchases would again be made in Israel. In other words, a surrounding army is there, and Jeremiah goes out and buys some real estate. Not only was this a short-term prophecy, but it was picked up later in the New Testament as having a larger significance.

Judas betrayed Jesus for thirty pieces of silver, as Zechariah had predicted (Zech. 11:12–13). Though he returned the money to the priests who had given it to him, they were hyper-scrupulous about putting it back into the account because it was blood money. It was acceptable to take innocent blood, but you had to keep the right money in the right accounts. Otherwise, God might be displeased. Consequently, they bought a field with it (presumably in Judas' name, for it was his money), and it was called a field of blood. Jeremiah bought a field for silver (32:6–9), and the import of this is stated in verse 44. "Fields shall be bought for money" ("for silver," NIV). When Matthew refers to this, he conflates the prophecies from Zechariah and Jeremiah, but he is referring to the same event. This was the price at which the Lord was valued by them. This is clearly in the context of judgment, which fell on Judas and on Jerusalem again, but it is woven together with a series of promises also. God promises to bring them back from exile (32:37), and he says, "And they shall be my people, and I will be their God" (32:38). This statement is also made in Leviticus 26:12 and in Ezekiel 37:27, and is quoted by Paul in 2 Corinthians 6:16. This is clearly talking about the glories of the New Covenant, which is particularly plain in Ezekiel. But Paul puts it beyond all doubt. "What agreement has the temple of God with idols? For we are the temple of the living God; as God said, 'I will make my dwelling among them and walk among them, and I will be their God, and they shall be my people' " (2 Cor. 6:16).

In this section of Jeremiah, therefore, we have dual prophecies of judgment and grace. Judas, as a type of unbelieving Israel, dies in a field of blood—bought with silver. Jerusalem in the days of Jeremiah was under siege and the Jerusalem of Christ's day was going to have the same thing happen to it.

At the same time, a glorious new beginning was promised. A new city was going to be established, and this New Jerusalem could not be taken down because of Babylonians or Romans. "It shall not be uprooted or overthrown anymore forever" (31:40). The reason the New Jerusalem could not be destroyed or uprooted is because it was founded on a better covenant, one that dealt with the heart of man. This was to be an *everlasting* covenant (32:40).

The first covenant had a problem—the people who had entered into covenant with God. "For if that first covenant had been faultless, there would have been no occasion to look for a second. For he finds fault with *them* when he says . . ." (Heb. 8:7–8a, emphasis mine). The discussion of Jeremiah's promise begins with the fact that the older covenant had failed because the nature of the people in it was not dealt with. The coming New Covenant therefore had to correct this deficiency, which it did.

So the writer of Hebrews quotes the entire promise from Jeremiah in Hebrews 8:8b–12 and returns to this two chapters later, quoting an abridged form of that passage which reveals how God fixed the problem. He saw to it that his holy law was inscribed in their minds and hearts (Heb. 10:16) and he ensured that their sins would be completely forgiven (Heb. 10:17). That is how the people are changed—the law is internalized, and their sins are forgiven once for all, not requiring the ongoing mechanism of a sacrificial system.

This can be (and has been) applied woodenly. By assuming that there is an absolute and essential difference between the two covenants, and that this can be expressed in terms of external and internal, as though God were only concerned for external conformity in the Old Covenant, but in the New Covenant, he somehow started caring about the heart. Of course, Old Testament saints could have the law inscribed on their hearts, and Old Testament saints could have their sins forgiven. So how is this a distinguishing feature of the New Covenant?

There are two points to make here—one negative and one positive. The negative point is that we cannot interpret these citations in Hebrews in such a way as to make nonsense of all the other exhortations of Hebrews. In other words, if "they shall all know me" means that every last covenant member is elect, and that absolutely no one can fall from that electing grace, then what on earth was the book written *for*, then? If the author of Hebrews is trying to teach us here that a New Covenant member cannot sin in this way, then why does he appear to be so worried?

The positive point can be made this way. The internalization of the law and the forgiveness of sins were established definitively *in history* by the death and resurrection of Jesus Christ. Because of this, it will never be necessary for God to send another Son, another sacrifice, another way. Christ suffered once for all, and he rose from the dead, once for all. Because of this, the blessings of the older covenant (which a minority of those covenant members actually enjoyed) were now established within the covenant, ensuring that more and more covenant members would come to possess them in truth.

I don't believe these are the actual numbers, but let me just use them for purposes of illustration. Let us suppose that throughout the course of the Old Testament five percent of the Jews were genuine believers and ninety-five percent were reprobate. And let us say that as the result of Christ's triumph and his gift of the Holy Spirit to the church, in the time of the New Testament five percent were reprobate and ninety-five percent were elect. This difference was accomplished by the sacrifice of Jesus, which displaced the older sacrificial system. It was a difference that was accomplished in time and in history.

At the same time, the warnings that applied to the ninety-five percent in the Old Testament would still apply, straight across, to the five percent in the New Testament. The enjoyment by faith of all God's promises that Abraham and numerous other saints had in the Old Testament are now enjoyed by many more people because God's Spirit has been *poured* out.

Part Two

Commentary on Hebrews

4

The Glory of Christ

In a very real way, the tragedy of modern worship is that we have become like the Samaritans—we worship what we do not know. The grief of our era is that the church has fallen into the worship of a tiny Christ. And a good portion of the needed remedy is to be found in the book of Hebrews.

> Long ago, at many times and in many ways, God spoke to our fathers by the prophets, but in these last days he has spoken to us by his Son, whom he appointed the heir of all things, through whom also he created the world. He is the radiance of the glory of God and the exact imprint of his nature, and he upholds the universe by the word of his power. After making purification for sins, he sat down at the right hand of the Majesty on high, having become as much superior to angels as the name he has inherited is more excellent than theirs. (Heb. 1:1–4)

We must come to see and know the supremacy of Christ, and the way we do this is through worshipping him. Our duty as Christians is to bear the name of Christ and to lift it up. This glorious book of Hebrews will instruct us in how we may best do this—the supremacy of Christ is a central theme of this epistle, a fact clearly demonstrated in this preamble.

How did God deal with us in "times past"? From the time of Adam to the Christ, God was not silent. Through the prophets, he spoke to us in different times and in different ways. But whether through dreams or visions, all the preparation was looking forward to the coming of Christ. Abraham rejoiced to the see the day of Christ because that was the direction he was looking. We rejoice that the day of Christ has come, and we look to him as well. Abraham believed God (vertically) and so he looked forward in history. We believe God (vertically) and so we look back in history to the advent of Christ, and as a consequence, we now look up in faith, where Christ is seated at the right hand of God the Father.

So we now have a final word. Christ has been spoken by God in these *last* days. Christ is, in a very important sense, God's *last* Word. After Christ, to expect a return to the "various times and various ways" of the Old Covenant is to disparage the glory of Christ. We see here that Christ was appointed by God to be the heir of all things. When Christ sent out his apostles to disciple the nations, it was based upon this inheritance, an inheritance already given and established. Christ owns it all already. Understanding this makes a great difference in our preaching—is the tone of our message one of begging or declaring? We are commissioned to declare to the world *an accomplished fact*. Christ is King. This is not a campaign to get everyone to vote for him so that he might become president at some future date. This is a word already spoken from heaven. All authority in heaven and on earth is in the palm of Jesus Christ. This means his inheritance includes Saudi Arabia, Israel, Canada, the United States, China, and Argentina. It all belongs to him already—he bought it with his blood. Why would he not take it?

Not only does Jesus possess all nations by right of redemption (which he certainly does), he also possesses them by right of creation. Christ is the creator of all things. Although the incarnation of

God becoming man begins in history, the Eternal Word did not begin in history. He is not part of creation; rather, he is the creator. The Eternal Word, the one who *spoke* the universe into existence from nothing, became Jesus, a man from Nazareth.

This Jesus, this man from God, this son of God, *the* Son of God, is the radiant glory of God himself. The one who has seen Christ has seen the Father, and the one who has seen Christ by faith has seen the Father by faith.

Christ is to the Father what light beams are to a light source. He streams from the Father eternally. The Father is the Light Source, and the Son is the Light Shining. And there never was a time when the Light was "off." How could there have been such a time? When headlights are over the crest of the hill, you can nevertheless see the "lume" of the light before you see the headlights themselves. When sailors are making landfall at night, they look for a lighthouse, still over the horizon. And before they see that lighthouse, they see the "lume" of the light from it. The Greek word for that kind of "lume" is the word used to describe Jesus here. Jesus is the effulgence of the glory of God.

Not only was the Word of God the agent of the creation of all things, he is also the agent who *sustains* all things today. Without him, everything around us would "vaporize" into nothingness. He did not create us and walk away. He created us and sustains us. He created the world and sustains it. He created countless galaxies and sustains them. And if he stopped sustaining, the material universe would go *poof*.

Still, the facts of creation and providence—so evident around us—do not bring us to acknowledge God. As my father once put it, the facts of "intelligent design" are a gross understatement. Yet men still stare at the glory around them, blind to it. This is because of sin, and so Christ stoops from his creational glory, and adopts an even greater glory, a redemptive glory, a glory that was flogged and nailed to a piece of wood. Christ is the savior of the world, the redeemer of his people, and he was born to die. The fact of God becoming man was not a self-contained miracle, and still less was it just to enable us to tell a sentimental story about a baby in a manger. His incarnation was teleological—Christ came to do the will of the Father, and that will was for him to die for all the sins of all his people. His birth had a purpose, and that purpose was to give him a body which was capable of dying.

Because of his victory over the grave, Christ is now seated at the right hand of his Father, not for rest, *but for rule*. He is to reign from there until his enemies are made his footstool. Heaven must receive him, must hold him, until all is subdued in his name through the preaching of the gospel. Only then will he return, and destroy the last remaining enemy, which is death.

From all this, we see how much greater than the angels Christ is. He is no created Christ. He is no tiny Christ. He is not just an *arch*-archangel. An undue exaltation of angels was an easy mistake for the first-century Jews to make (and many of them did make it). An important purpose of this first chapter of Hebrews is to show the supremacy of Christ over these angels, because some of that superstitious reverence for angels had begun to creep into the church. But our Lord's name is far above all angels, all principalities and powers. His name is a most excellent name, for unto us a child is born. His name is to be adored forever, for unto us a son is given. His name shall be honored by all who love true authority, for the government shall be upon his shoulder. His name shall be called Wonderful, Counselor, the Mighty God, the Everlasting Father, the Prince of all Peace. His name shall be blessed from the river to the end of the earth precisely because of the increase of his government, and of peace there will never be an end. His name shall be Jesus, the son of David, for he will sit upon the throne of his father David until the consummation of all things. His name will be called royal and majestic for he will order his kingdom, and establish it with judgment and justice forever. This, the prophet Isaiah promised us, will be accomplished by the zeal of the Lord of hosts himself. And we now, living on the other side of this staggering fulfillment, can rest in the fact that the zeal of the Lord of hosts has *already* performed it.

THE OIL OF GLADNESS

The author of Hebrews is seeking to show his Jewish readers that Christ's supremacy includes supremacy over every angelic being. As already mentioned, an undue regard for angels was common among the Jews of this period, and the author of Hebrews is taking care to lift the name of Christ above *every* name. He accomplishes this through a chain of quotations from the Old Testament (Heb. 1:5–9):

> For to which of the angels did God ever say,
>
> "You are my Son,
> today I have begotten you"?
>
> Or again,
>
> "I will be to him a father,
> and he shall be to me a son"?
>
> And again, when he brings the firstborn into the world, he says,
>
> "Let all God's angels worship him."
>
> Of the angels he says,
>
> "He makes his angels winds,
> and his ministers a flame of fire."
>
> But of the Son he says,
>
> "Your throne, O God, is forever and ever,
> the scepter of uprightness is the scepter of your kingdom.
> You have loved righteousness and hated wickedness;
> therefore God, your God, has anointed you
> with the oil of gladness beyond your companions."

Christ is the begotten son. The first quotation here is from Psalm 2. This is a clear reference to the resurrection of Christ from the dead, which we learn from the psalm itself and from how Paul quotes the same passage elsewhere. This is the argumentative position the phrase occupies in the original psalm, and this is the application Paul makes of it in Acts 13:33. What God promised, he fulfilled through the resurrection of Jesus, as spoken of in Psalm 2. So the begetting here is *from the dead*, as Paul speaks in Colossians 1:18.

If we look up all the New Testament quotations from Psalm 2, we find out that the opening lines are quoted with reference to the crucifixion of Jesus. "Why did the Gentiles rage?" (Acts 4:25). The heathen plot in verses 1 through 3. God laughs at them and rebukes them in verses 4 through 6. So what is the next thing that happens? The resurrection—"today I have begotten you." And immediately after the resurrection, God gives all the nations to Christ as his blood-bought inheritance—which is a theme of a good portion of the rest of this epistle. But Paul puts the matter beyond dispute when he says, "This he has fulfilled to us their children *by raising Jesus*, as also it is written in the second Psalm, 'You are my Son, *today I have begotten you*' " (Acts 13:33).

This means the expression here of Christ's "being begotten" should not be confused with John's expression "only-begotten," which has special reference to Christ's eternal relationship to the Father, and not to his earthly birth or his resurrection. Christ is begotten *from the dead* and so all the nations of men belong to him.

He reigns over these nations as the rightful heir of David. Christ reigns as the Son of David. God had promised David that his seed would reign forever, a promise found in 2 Samuel 7:14. Some of it clearly applies to his sinful descendants like Solomon (i.e., "If he commits iniquity . . ."), but as the author of Hebrews makes plain, the final and ultimate fulfillment of this promise is found in Christ. This is the throne of David, occupied by Christ. Christ is the king of the world because of the resurrection and not as a result of the second coming. Christ is king *now*, and not just later.

Being in this position, he is the one that angels worship. When Christ is brought into the world (i.e., as a *man*), God commands the angels to *worship* him. He is clearly greater than they are, but how much greater? This command is found addressed to the gods in Psalm 97:7, and in the Septuagint the command is addressed to angels in Deuteronomy 32:43. This object of angelic worship is a *Davidson*. Because of the incarnation, where Christ became man, the angels are summoned to worship the God/man, which means that they must not and cannot be seen as greater than man. They are servants of man.

So what are these angels? Psalm 104:4 tells us that they are creatures and servants—spirits, ministers, and flames of fire. Because God is growing man up to maturity in Christ, our angelic servants were much more impressive to us when we were spiritual toddlers in the Old Covenant, under the care of these, our spiritual nurses. But now in the new creation, mankind in Christ has dominion over all things, including the angels. The psalm quoted makes it very plain that these angels were and are part of the created order of things (winds and fire), over which God reigns. But there is more to it than this.

God has always exercised divine sovereignty over all things (atoms, hairs on head, sparrows falling to the ground). But now we are talking about something quite different—we are talking about the *mediatorial reign* of Christ, the resurrected man, and the reign with him of all who have faith in him. He has made us kings and priests. The mediators in the Old Covenant were angels. The mediator and prince in the New Covenant is a man, and men who have faith in him extend the manifestation of his kingdom through preaching the gospel and faithful worship. God is rebuilding the entire human race in Christ. We wrecked the human race in Adam, and God decided to renovate the house. But he decided to renovate the house while we were all still living in it.

So then God himself speaks, addressing the son. *To the son*, God says, "Your throne, *O God* . . ." The force of these words is inescapable. For those who would deny the deity of Christ, these are among the most embarrassing words in the Bible. God himself speaks to the Son, calling him *God*. No refuge can be found in Greek grammar, though many seek it there. With all due respect for Dr. Johnson, patriotism is not the last refuge of the scoundrel—that honored position would belong to Greek word studies. Because he is God, Christ's throne is eternal. But remember, this is also the throne of *David*. In addition, the scepter of righteousness is the scepter of his kingdom; Christ reigns according to his character; the standard of his kingdom is *not* relative. It does not vary or fluctuate, any more than he does. Our Lord Christ loves righteousness, and he hates lawlessness; Christ is our supreme ruler, and Christ loves and hates. Our lives should reflect our understanding of this.

If we do not love as he loves, we do not love. If we do not learn to hate as he does (hating lawlessness), then we do not know the meaning of love. All who love the Lord hate evil (Prov. 8:13). Therefore, God's *God* has anointed him with the oil of gladness. As the *Christ*, he is the anointed one. This is what *Christ* and *Messiah* mean.

At the same time, it is the oil of *gladness*. Where did Christians get the idea that goodness slouches around with a long face? Christ is our king and he reigns. He loves righteousness and he hates lawlessness. Those with long faces are revealing to the world far more than they know. Christians must live as though they serve a *triumphant* King Jesus—for they actually do. Fussy Christians, prim and proper Christians, "tsk"ing Christians, sentimental Christians, schoolmarmish Christians, keep-off-the-grass Christians—all need to go and learn what the oil of gladness refers to. Because he has received the oil of gladness, he is the Christ. Now we are Christians—we share his name, and the power of his anointing is ours as well. But again, it is the oil of *gladness*.

YOU ARE MY SON

We have already looked at Psalm 2 in Hebrews, but we need to take a closer look now. The Psalm 2 provides us with a textbook case on how New Testament quotations can shed a brilliant light on the contexts of an Old Testament passage (Ps. 2:1–12, NKJV):

> Why do the nations rage,
>   And the people plot a vain thing?
> The kings of the earth set themselves,
>   And the rulers take counsel together,
>   Against the LORD and against His Anointed, *saying*,
> "Let us break Their bonds in pieces
> And cast away Their cords from us."
>
> He who sits in the heavens shall laugh;
>   The LORD shall hold them in derision.
> Then He shall speak to them in His wrath,
>   And distress them in His deep displeasure:
> "Yet I have set My King

On My holy hill of Zion."

"I will declare the decree:
The LORD has said to Me,
'You *are* My Son,
Today I have begotten You.
Ask of Me, and I will give *You*
The nations *for* Your inheritance,
And the ends of the earth *for* Your possession.
You shall break them with a rod of iron;
You shall dash them to pieces like a potter's vessel.' "

Now therefore, be wise, O kings;
Be instructed, you judges of the earth.
Serve the LORD with fear,
And rejoice with trembling.
Kiss the Son, lest He be angry,
And you perish *in* the way,
When His wrath is kindled but a little.
Blessed *are* all those who put their trust in Him."

This psalm is quoted all over the place, one of the more important places being in Acts 4, pointing to the crucifixion.

And when they heard it, they lifted their voices together to God and said, "Sovereign Lord, who made the heaven and the earth and the sea and everything in them, who through the mouth of our father David, your servant, said by the Holy Spirit,

'Why did the Gentiles rage,
and the peoples plot in vain?
The kings of the earth set themselves,
and the rulers were gathered together,
against the Lord and against his Anointed'—

for truly in this city there were gathered together against your holy servant Jesus, whom you anointed, both Herod and Pontius Pilate, along with the Gentiles and the peoples of Israel, to do whatever your hand and your plan had predestined to take place." (Acts 4:24–28)

This citation establishes that the psalm is in fact about Christ, and that the first few verses are a prophecy of his crucifixion. Verse 7 of the psalm is quoted three times in the New Testament, and all three to the same effect. Note the italicized phrases.

First—God has fulfilled this for us in that *he has raised* up Jesus. *As it is also written* in the second psalm: "You are my Son, today I have begotten you" (Acts 13:33).

Second—having become so much better than the angels, as he has *by inheritance obtained a more excellent name* than they. "For to which of the angels did God ever say: 'You are my Son, today I have begotten you'?" (Heb. 1:5a).

Third—so also Christ did not glorify himself *to become High Priest*, but it was he who said to him: "You are my Son, today I have begotten you" (Heb. 5:5).

In other words, the prophecy "You are my Son . . ." is God's declaration that Christ is his son (cf. Rom. 1:4). It is also God investing Christ with the office of High Priest and is a declaration that he makes at, and by means of, the resurrection of Christ.

Now God has given universal dominion to Christ, and to all those who are *in* Christ. What does it say to those who are in Christ? "Only hold fast what you have until I come. The one who conquers and who keeps my works until the end, to him I will give authority over the nations, and he will rule them with a *rod of iron*, as when earthen pots are broken in pieces, even as I myself have received authority from my Father. And I will give him the morning star" (Rev. 2:25–28).

What does it say to Christ himself? "He is clothed in a robe dipped in blood, and the name by which he is called is The Word of God. And the armies of heaven, arrayed in fine linen, white and pure, were following him on white horses. From his mouth comes a sharp sword with which to strike down the nations, and he will rule them with a *rod of iron*. He will tread the winepress of the fury of the wrath of God the Almighty" (Rev. 19:13–15).

WORSHIP AS THE KEY TO HISTORY

We have already seen the great theme of Christ's supremacy over the angels. Here in this passage, his greatness is declared in his work of creating and dissolving all created things, and also in his mediatorial reign.

> And,
>
> "You, Lord, laid the foundation of the earth in the beginning,
> and the heavens are the work of your hands;
> they will perish, but you remain;
> they will all wear out like a garment,
> like a robe you will roll them up,
> like a garment they will be changed.
> But you are the same,
> and your years will have no end."
>
> And to which of the angels has he ever said,
>
> "Sit at my right hand
> until I make your enemies a footstool for your feet"?
>
> Are they not all ministering spirits sent out to serve for the sake of those who are to inherit salvation? (Heb. 1:10–14)

This passage begins with an *and*, which shows us that God the Father is still speaking to the Son. Remember that earlier God addressed the Son *as God*; here he addresses him as creator. The Word of God did the concrete work of laying the foundation of the earth, and he was the one who did the finished work in the heavens. The New Testament tells us repeatedly that the Word of God, the second person of the Trinity, is the agent of all creation. And God said, "Let there be light . . ." What is the Word of God but God speaking, and when God spoke (through the Son) in this particular way, the universe came to be. Consider also John 1:3, Colossians 1:16, and verse 2 of this chapter. As creator, therefore, Christ is God, and much greater than the angels.

He is also the dissolver. In verse 3, we learned that Christ sustains all created things; here we are told that he will not always do so. The heavens and earth which he created are things which wear out. The same processes which undo your favorite pair of jeans will also undo the heavens and earth. The created order, as it is now, will perish. Christ never alters, never changes. He is always the same, and his years will never fail, but the created order as it is now will perish. However, remember God's way. Death is followed by resurrection. Christ will fold it all up, but then it will then be transformed. This shows us that the creation will not be annihilated, but it will grow old, it will be folded up, and then it will be transformed, and Christ will do it all. This can be identified with the glory the creation will receive when we are revealed as the sons of God at the resurrection (Rom. 8). Just as we will receive a new body, so the universe around us will receive a new body.

So Christ is king. The author repeats his question. To which of the angels did God ever say anything like this? The nature of the question (and the nature of angels) indicates that the glory of sitting at God's right hand is immeasurable. Countless sermons could be preached on this text alone.

"*Sit at my right hand . . .*": Christ is not sitting there to rest, or to recuperate, but to reign. What is the right hand of God but the place of all authority? And if Christ was the agent of creation, what will he do now as the agent of re-creation?

"*until I make . . .*": Christ is reigning *now*, and he will continue to reign until his will is fully accomplished. He did not leave in order that his will would not be done. He left and assumed the position of all rule and authority, over every nation and tribe, and he will continue to sit at the right hand of the Father *until* . . . In other words, while Christ is seated there, before his return, all his enemies (with death the only exception) will be subdued to him. This will be through the means that he ordained, which is the preaching of the gospel. Through the declaration of Christ's mediatorial lordship, and the basis of it, which is his death and resurrection, everything will be put right.

"*your enemies . . .*": Christ is being spoken of here as king, and these enemies are any enemies of his kingdom. The fact that Christ is reigning does not mean that he has no enemies. It means he has those enemies well in hand. The devil's capital city has fallen, and the proclamation of the gospel throughout the world is the mopping-up operation in the hinterlands. In these outlying areas, there are still enemies to Christ's kingdom. There are still those who say, "We do not want this man to rule over us." That's too bad.

"*a footstool for your feet . . .*": Christ's enemies, all of them, will be subdued and brought under his visible authority. They are under his authority *now*; this will be made manifest to all so that it is beyond dispute. Christ is Lord; the time is coming when every tongue will confess that he is Lord, and every knee will bow. But this is so important—we do not confess that he is Lord as the means of making him Lord. He *is* Lord, and over time his lordship will be manifested through the fact that the whole earth confesses it. We are preaching and announcing and declaring an accomplished fact. The earth was going around the sun before people started believing Copernicus.

If Christ is so much greater than the angels, then, what is the role of angels? We must not make the mistake of over-reacting by assigning no biblical role whatever to angels. They are fellow servants and not to be worshipped. However, their liturgical ministry—work in the course of the church—is important. They are sent forth. They stand in the presence of God, and God sends them to minister to us. They minister to those who will inherit salvation. They minister to the Christian church. By faith, we belong to the same company of worshippers as they do. In coming into the New Jerusalem, which is the Christian church, we have also come into an innumerable company of angels (Heb. 12:22). All things, whether in heaven or on earth, have been reconciled in Christ (Col. 1:20). This means that they are servants in the divine household, ministering to the sons of the house, but as such, they are still honored members of the house.

Our response should be gratitude and faith, not vain speculations. Our rule is to be the Word alone. But Scripture does give us some idea what the ministry of these angels in part consists of. First, they protect us from danger. "The angel of the LORD encamps around those who fear him" (Ps. 34:7). Secondly, another responsibility is to witness our obedience, sufferings, and worship. The apostle Paul was a spectacle both before angels and men (1 Cor. 4:9). Timothy was charged before the elect angels to discharge his ministerial duties (1 Tim. 5:21). The modesty and decorum of women in public assembly is important "because of the angels" (1 Cor. 11:10).

Third, they escort us from this life: ". . . and was carried by the angels to Abraham's side" (Luke 16:22). And last, they are responsible to attend us at the day of resurrection: "When the Son of Man comes in his glory, and all the angels with him, then he will sit on his glorious throne" (Matt. 25:31).

However, all this service which the angels render to the church is not the kind of service which would make us worship them. The service that Christ rendered to the church—by offering up his life, by submitting to burial, by rising from the dead, by ascending into heaven to receive the crown of all nations—is service that makes us aware of our need to worship him. And as we worship God the Father through our worship of God the Son, in the power of God the Holy Spirit, the world is transformed. The key to world history is right worship.

ALL ENDS OF EARTH

The book of Psalms is one of the most postmillennial books in the Bible. The statements we find there are awfully difficult to get around. So why even try?

> My God, My God, why have You forsaken Me?
> Why are You so far from helping Me,
> And from the words of My groaning?
>
> . . . .
>
> They divide My garments among them,
> And for My clothing they cast lots.
>
> . . . .
>
> I will declare Your name to My brethren;

In the midst of the assembly I will praise You.
You who fear the LORD, praise Him!
All you descendants of Jacob, glorify Him,
And fear Him, all you offspring of Israel!
For He has not despised nor abhorred the affliction of the afflicted;
Nor has He hidden His face from Him;
But when He cried to Him, He heard.

My praise *shall be* of You in the great assembly;
I will pay My vows before those who fear Him.
The poor shall eat and be satisfied;
Those who seek Him will praise the LORD.
Let your heart live forever!

All the ends of the world shall remember and turn to the LORD,
And all the families of the nations
Shall worship before You.
For the kingdom *is* the LORD's,
And He rules over the nations.

All the prosperous of the earth
Shall eat and worship;
All those who go down to the dust
Shall bow before Him,
Even he who cannot keep himself alive.

A posterity shall serve Him.
It will be recounted of the Lord to the *next* generation,
They will come and declare His righteousness to a people who will be born,
That He has done this. (Ps. 22:1–31, NKJV)

This psalm is quoted in three places in the New Testament. The first verse is quoted in Matthew 27:46 together with Mark 15:34. The eighteenth verse is quoted in John 19:24. The twenty-second verse is quoted in Hebrews 2:12, which is our main interest here. As with Psalm 2, these quotations frame the entire argument of the psalm.

Jesus quotes the first verse of this psalm from the cross. "And about the ninth hour Jesus cried out with a loud voice, saying, 'Eli,

Eli, lema sabachthani?' that is, 'My God, my God, why have you forsaken me?' " (Matt. 27:46). And then in Mark: "And at the ninth hour Jesus cried with a loud voice, 'Eloi, Eloi, lema sabachthani?' which means, 'My God, my God, why have you forsaken me?' " (Mark 15:34).

Note three things about this cry of despair. The first is that even when forsaken by God, Jesus never sinned. It is still "*my* God." Second, even at the point of despair, Jesus quotes the Scripture. And third, he quoted a Scripture which ends in postmillennial triumph. In short, it was unique despair—despair full of hope. As the author of Hebrews notes—"looking to Jesus, the founder and perfecter of *our* faith, who for the joy that was set before him endured the cross, despising the shame, and is seated at the right hand of the throne of God" (Heb. 12:2).

The second quotation comes in John 19:24. "So they said to one another, 'Let us not tear it, but cast lots for it to see whose it shall be.' This was to fulfill the Scripture which says, 'They divided my garments among them, and for my clothing they cast lots.' So the soldiers did these things." This tells us that this portion of the psalm is describing certain physical features of the crucifixion. Other comparable features not *expressly* quoted in the New Testament are mockery he endured (vv. 6–8), bones out of joint (v. 14), dogs surrounding him (v. 16), hands and feet pierced (v. 16), and bones counted (v. 17).

The Lord cries out for deliverance in verses 19 through 21. In verse 22, we see his statement of triumph, which is quoted as such in Hebrews 2:12. But look back at verse 9. This is clearly a statement about Christ's identifying with his brethren. And so what is the result of this conquest on the cross? We find in the concluding verses of this psalm one of the most powerful statements of eschatological hope found anywhere in Scripture, and that hope is expressly quoted in the book of Hebrews. Consider what *will* happen. God has not despised the sacrifice of his Son (v. 24); the whole earth *will* turn to God (v. 27); all the families in the world *will* worship him (v. 27). Everyone *will* serve him, and this *will* be done by God (v. 31).

5

Stricter Sanctions

We have now come to the first great warning of this epistle. As the force of the warning makes clear, this is not an exercise in academic theology. True theology is never merely academic. How we think is important to how we live, but how we think must never be taken as a substitute for how we live. Jesus tells us at the close of the Sermon on the Mount that hearing his words is not enough—if we put them into practice, we are building on a firm foundation. If we hear his words and refuse to obey him, then the house we are building is actually being built on spiritual sand. As Jesus was speaking those words, Herod was still in the process of building the temple on Moriah, on what he thought was a rock. The project was not yet completed, and Jesus gave his famous sermon on the Mount of Olives, and right across the way the sounds of construction could be heard in the distance. The Old Covenant temple was being built on sand, as the flood of Roman troops in 70 AD made plain. The promises of the New Covenant do not make it safe to build on sand, but rather promise that the people of God ultimately, in this covenant, will build on the Rock. But for those who pay no attention and build on sand regardless, the same thing happens to them as always has.

And so the book of Hebrews teaches us how to understand covenant warnings.

> Therefore we must pay much closer attention to what we have heard, lest we drift away from it. For since the message declared by angels proved to be reliable, and every transgression or disobedience received a just retribution, how shall we escape if we neglect such a great salvation? It was declared at first by the Lord, and it was attested to us by those who heard, while God also bore witness by signs and wonders and various miracles and by gifts of the Holy Spirit distributed according to his will. (Heb. 2:1–4)

The writer has been demonstrating the greatness of Christ over the angels, his supremacy over the entire created order. But the nature of this supremacy is important; the writer is not troubling us with arcane details of the celestial hierarchy. Christ is so much greater than the angels that we must guard against drifting away from him—this doctrine directly addresses our behavior; it is the foundation of our faithfulness. If the law, delivered through angels, was hedged and protected through just penalties, how much more will our great salvation be so protected through much more striking penalties? The word of the law proved steadfast; the gospel is also steadfast. The Lord spoke it first, those who heard the Lord also confirmed it, and God from heaven confirmed the message with miracles and gifts of the Holy Spirit. The miracles are signs and pointers showing something far greater; they are not to be sought after for their own sake. A wicked and adulterous generation seeks after a sign. A faithful generation reads the signs and goes beyond them to the thing signified. If a miracle is a great thing, how much greater is the Christ who is vouched for by the miracles? The person and work of the Lord Jesus Christ are to be the central objects of our attention.

Now here is the danger. These saints, the recipients of this exhortation, are warned against drifting away. In order to guard against this, it is necessary to give earnest heed. The problem is one of neglecting a great salvation, taking it for granted. While the crisis is one of a looming apostasy, this break with the faith has (seemingly) small beginnings. The careful reader is compelled to wonder—in what ways can modern Christians be sinfully resting, too at ease with what they know? Great unfaithfulness begins with small driftings. To receive a great salvation with less than the attention it merits is to be guilty of neglecting it, which is to treat it with contempt. How many Christians treat the message of salvation with a thoughtless contempt?

One of our great enemies in our walk with God is the force of gravity. It doesn't take a great deal of effort to stick to the ground, and the high jumping of genuine discipleship takes strenuous effort.

But God is not mocked. When he judges, in order to deliver his blow, he pushes against his revealed Word. He judges us for those things which he told us, and which we neglected. With the greater clarity of the New Covenant comes a greater strictness in judgment. In the New Covenant, covenantal judgments do not disappear. They are *greater*. Too many Christians have accepted the entirely unjustifiable notion that the New Covenant is a covenant without sanctions. In the older covenant, the thinking goes, there were strict sanctions. But in the New Covenant, God has decided to do the grace thing, and so there are no covenantal sanctions. The theory is quite pretty, and naturally comforting. The problem is that it collides with text after text after text, and especially in this book. The New Covenant has *stricter* sanctions, as we will repeatedly learn as we work our way through this epistle.

These are *covenant* warnings to *covenant* members. This is not primarily a warning against an unbeliever outside the church who fails to respond to the preaching of the gospel. The Bible does contain such warnings, but they are not in view here. This is a warning against members of the covenant community of God who are in danger of drifting away from it. Two points must be made here. First, the Bible plainly teaches that the elect (taken in the decretal, theological sense) *cannot* be separated from the love of God which is in Christ Jesus. No one can remove the elect from the Father's hand. If someone is genuinely regenerate, if he has been effectually called, then God *will* complete the good work which he has begun.

Secondly, nothing can be plainer than that there are professing Christians (who have some sort of genuine covenantal attachment to Christ) who can and will be removed from him because of unbelief. We have this warning here, we have Christ's warning in John 15, and we have Paul's in Romans 11. When this happens, such covenant members fall under the sanctions of the New Covenant, which bring a much stricter judgment.

Take someone who has confessed the name of Christ. The warning comes to him: Has he been paying earnest heed to the word of his great salvation? Has he been baptized into Christ's people? The warning comes to him: Has he been drifting away? Has he grown up among God's people? The warning comes to him: Has he neglected this message? Does he think that he will be protected by nodding his head? The conclusion of the matter is that we must pay earnest heed to *Christ*. We must never stop paying attention to the glory of his person and the worth of his work. To do anything else is the source of all spiritual sloth. And as we have seen here in this text, God judges all such sloth.

THE WORLD TO COME

The supremacy of Christ over the angels continues as the theme in the early portion of Hebrews, but with an important development within the text. Christ is not only supreme over the angels, he holds this position now as the Incarnate One—the God/man.

> Now it was not to angels that God subjected the world to come, of which we are speaking. It has been testified somewhere,
>
> "What is man, that you are mindful of him,
> or the son of man, that you care for him?
> You made him for a little while lower than the angels;
> you have crowned him with glory and honor,
> putting everything in subjection under his feet."

> Now in putting everything in subjection to him, he left nothing outside his control. At present, we do not yet see everything in subjection to him. But we see him who for a little while was made lower than the angels, namely Jesus, crowned with glory and honor because of the suffering of death, so that by the grace of God he might taste death for everyone. (Heb. 2:5–9)

The book of Hebrews is profoundly future-oriented. Because of who Jesus is, we may talk about the world to come with great confidence. Note what he says here—"the world to come, of which we are speaking." This is not a reference to heaven, or going to heaven when we die; it is a reference to the coming Christian aeon. The word here for world refers to the inhabited earth. The Judaic aeon was coming to a close and was fading away. There would be a cataclysmic finish to that age in the destruction of the temple in 70 AD. But in the world to come, the authority which angelic beings had in the Old Testament was transferred to Christ, and, as we will see, to all of mankind considered *in Christ*.

In defense of this idea, the author of Hebrews cites Psalm 8. Now two great truths emerge from this psalm. The first is the greatness of God over all things, and the obvious insignificance of man. "What is man that you are mindful of him . . ." The second is the fact that this great God has bestowed mind-boggling greatness on insignificant man: "*crowned* with glory and honor . . ." How was this done? The biblical answer is that it was done *in and through Christ*.

When we consider Psalm 8, it is clear that David is speaking clearly about *mankind*. The psalm is not *directly* messianic (although it should be clear that the entire Psalter is messianic at some level). At the same time, the author of Hebrews clearly connects it with Christ. Man is given universal dominion over all things, but this dominion does not come to fruition apart from Christ. Because of our sin in Adam, we were crippled in our ability to exercise that dominion. This inability, this impotence, is healed in Christ. All Scriptures are about Christ, because they all involve mankind in some way, shape, or form. Christ is Mankind.

Now the Christian faith is a *historical* faith. Above we saw that we are talking about the "world to come." We do not *yet* see everything subject to man. We know that bringing man to maturity is a central part of God's plan for us. As man is brought to maturity in Christ, his relationship to the world around him will be gradually transformed.

Although the author of Hebrews did not see mankind's dominion over all things with his eyes, he *did* see it in the promises of God. And all God's promises are fulfilled in Christ. In Christ, all the promises are *yes* and *amen*. We do not *yet* see everything in subjection to mankind. But, in the gospel, we see Christ by faith. These are some of the things we must consider by faith.

"But we see him . . . namely Jesus . . ." This is not mysticism, but faith. Consider the phrase "made him for a little while lower than the angels." This is a reference to the fact that in Christ God was *enfleshed*. "And the Word became flesh and dwelt among us, and we have seen his glory, glory as of the only Son from the Father, full of grace and truth" (John 1:14). Who is the antichrist, and who has a spirit of falsehood? The one who denies that Jesus is come *in the flesh* (1 John 4:2).

"[*B*]*ecause of the suffering of death . . .*" Christ died on the cross as a perfect substitute for his people. This is the heart of the gospel. The cross is the glory of Christianity—it is there that Christ redeemed his people and conquered his enemies.

"[*C*]*rowned with glory and honor . . .*" After Christ's death, God raised him from the dead and crowned him with glory and all honor. All authority has been given to him. Notice that this is the phrase used earlier of mankind in Psalm 8. *Man* is crowned with glory and honor which we do not yet see. We *do* see Jesus crowned with glory and honor *on our behalf*. Christ has been raised, exalted, enthroned, and made ruler and sovereign. In faith, we should think about him in this position, and as we do, we will come to understand the future nature of man. *Christ* is the future nature of man.

"[*S*]*o that by the grace of God he might taste death for everyone.*" Christ's redemption was not for a tiny handful of people. The elect are not a narrow trickle of forgiven sinners barely making it into heaven. Remember, we are speaking of "the world to come." The world to come, in the Christian aeon, is not subject to angels, but rather to mankind *in Christ*. Christ tasting death for everyone does not mean that he tried to save Judas and Pharaoh in his dying, but failed at it. Still less can it mean that he died for a mere fifteen or sixteen people, and successfully secured their salvation. God sent his Son into the world *to save the world* (John 3:17).

As we grow in our understanding of the gospel, and grow in our knowledge of what it was that Jesus came to do, we will grow up into that image. As we look at Christ in faith, we are transformed from one degree of glory to another. And this means that we learn to restore the created order around us. This is not a promise concerning the nature of heaven after we die. This is a promise about the future history of our world, the world we are currently living in. As we grow up into Christ, and as Christ grows in us, we see more and more of the disordered world coming back into order, more and more fractures mended. The only disorder in the world that will not be dealt with this way, prior to the second coming of Christ, will be death itself. *That* enemy will fall at the word of Christ himself, spoken at his return. All other enemies will be subdued, and the instrument for doing this will be the gospel proclaimed by mankind in Christ to that ever-decreasing portion of mankind outside of Christ. So death will not be destroyed until the second coming. Prior to that, the children will play with cobras.

WHAT IS MAN?

In this psalm we find the answer to the perennial question, "What is man?" The answer given in the Bible is that *Christ* is man. Now what is *that* supposed to mean?

> O LORD, our Lord,
>   how majestic is your name in all the earth!
> You have set your glory above the heavens.
>   Out of the mouth of babies and infants,
> you have established strength because of your foes,
>   to still the enemy and the avenger.
>
> When I look at your heavens, the work of your fingers,
>   the moon and the stars, which you have set in place,
> what is man that you are mindful of him,

> and the son of man that you care for him?
> Yet you have made him a little lower than the heavenly beings
> and crowned him with glory and honor.
> You have given him dominion over the works of your hands;
> you have put all things under his feet,
> all sheep and oxen,
> and also the beasts of the field,
> the birds of the heavens, and the fish of the sea,
> whatever passes along the paths of the seas.
>
> O LORD, our Lord,
> how majestic is your name in all the earth! (Ps. 8:1–9)

This psalm is quoted three times in the New Testament. The first quotation is in Matthew 21:16, where the Lord Jesus quotes it against the chief priests and scribes. The second set of quotations is found in eschatological passages—Hebrews 2:6 and following and 1 Corinthians 15:27. All the quotations apply the psalm to Jesus Christ. But this does not mean that the psalm does not apply to all mankind—far from it. It applies fully to the new humanity that God has now established in Christ Jesus.

The first citation applies the words about infants and children to the response of the kids to Christ's entry into Jerusalem. "But when the chief priests and the scribes saw the wonderful things that he did, and the children crying out in the temple, 'Hosanna to the Son of David!' they were indignant, and they said to him, 'Do you hear what these are saying?' And Jesus said to them, 'Yes; have you never read, "Out of the mouth of infants and nursing babies you have prepared praise"?' " (Matt. 21:15–16). This praise by the children identifies Christ as the subject of the psalm, but must not be detached from the subject matter of the rest of the psalm, which is clearly the dominion of mankind. More about this in a moment.

The eschatological quotations of this psalm bring everything into focus. The world is to be recreated in the second Adam, the second Man.

> Now it was not to angels that God subjected the world to come, of which we are speaking. It has been testified somewhere,

> "What is man, that you are mindful of him,
> or the son of man, that you care for him?
> You made him for a little while lower than the angels;
> you have crowned him with glory and honor,
> putting everything in subjection under his feet."
>
> Now in putting everything in subjection to him, he left nothing outside his control. At present, we do not yet see everything in subjection to him. But we see him who for a little while was made lower than the angels, namely Jesus, crowned with glory and honor because of the suffering of death, so that by the grace of God he might taste death for everyone. (Heb. 2:5–9)

Put simply, although the creation is not visibly subject to mankind, we *do* see Jesus as the fulfillment of this. In other words, we see this psalm fulfilled in Christ by faith, and then as a consequence of that faith, we will come to see all things brought under the control of man. We do not *yet* see everything in subjection to man, but we will eventually see it with our eyes as the gospel continues to go out into the world.

Paul makes this explicit in his citation of Psalm 8. "For he must reign until he has put all his enemies under his feet. The last enemy to be destroyed is death. For 'God has put all things in subjection under his feet.' But when it says, 'all things are put in subjection,' it is plain that he is excepted who put all things in subjection under him. When all things are subjected to him, then the Son himself will also be subjected to him who put all things in subjection under him, that God may be all in all" (1 Cor. 15:25–28). Here Paul quotes Psalm 8 in conjunction with Psalm 110, which is quoted in multiple places throughout Hebrews. The New Testament not only teaches us that these two psalms are fulfilled in Christ, but also that they are fulfilled together. This Pauline interpretation explicitly states that the "feet" in question are Christ's. Christ must reign in heaven until the words of the psalm are literally true concerning all of the new mankind, who are, as the body of Christ, the feet of Christ.

THE CAPTAIN OF OUR SALVATION

We must never forget the central theme of this book, which is the supremacy of Christ over all his rivals. In this next verse, we need to consider the supremacy of Christ in his authority to *save*. "For it was fitting that he, for whom and by whom all things exist, in bringing many sons to glory, should make the founder of their salvation perfect through suffering" (Heb. 2:10).

By the grace of God, Christ tasted death for everyone. This is because it was fitting for him (that is, God) to equip the Son of God to be our Savior. This God is the one *for* whom everything exists, and the one *by* whom everything exists. The task he is accomplishing is the bringing of many sons into glory—the glory of Christ is not given to him in isolation. He is glorified as *our* forerunner. As God equipped him to be our Savior, he did this by establishing him through suffering, making him therefore the captain of our salvation.

Salvation is to the glory of God. All who acknowledge that God created everything know that everything exists by him. But not all Christians know why everything was created—everything exists *for* him as well. We live, breath, walk, talk, *and come to salvation* in order that God's name might be lifted up. It is fitting for God, *for* whom all exists, to bring *us* to salvation. Our salvation is ordered to his glory, just like everything else.

So the ultimate purpose of all things is the glory of God. This must never be forgotten. But God's purpose is to bring *many* sons to glory. How can this be reconciled? The answer will be beyond us if we think of God as just "another character in the play." The glory given to us in Christ is not glory taken away from him. This is not a zero-sum game. In the grace of God, *glory grows*. As we come to salvation, and share in his glory, it magnifies his glory. His glory, already infinite, overflows some more. Further, remember that before the process began, God was not deficient in glory. He was meeting no need within himself when he created the universe for his own glory. He was correcting no problems. The glory that comes to his name through our salvation is true glory, and it is superfluous glory. God wastes glory, throwing it all over the place.

When it comes to grace and glory, our triune God is a prodigal spendthrift.

We must also consider the phrase "should make . . . perfect through suffering." Was Christ imperfect before he was made perfect? Did God have to sanctify him from sin? The answer is clearly *no*. The author of Hebrews later tells us that although Christ was tempted, he was completely without sin. So what does this mean? The word in the original means to "consecrate" or "dedicate" or "set apart" to a particular office. Christ did not rise above "sinfulness" as he was made perfect; rather, he was ordained to be the captain of our salvation as he was fitted or equipped to that office. His sufferings were his preparation to ordination as our *captain*.

The word *captain* is very interesting. That word means prince, ruler, or captain. "Behold, I made him a witness to the peoples, a leader and commander for the peoples" (Is. 55:4). In our salvation, Christ is our prince. Not to put too fine a point on it, this means that he tells us what to do. We serve him as he brings us to glory.

The point of application is obvious. If Christ is not your captain, he is not the captain of your salvation. Those who want to sever Christ in his offices, making him Savior at one point, and Lord at another, are tampering with the gospel in a fearful way. Christ as our prince does not have perfect subjects (this is not what his captaincy means), but he does wield a perfect authority over those whom he is bringing into salvation.

CHRIST THE SINGER

The Bible teaches us that when Christ brings us to heaven, he does not do so while holding his nose. Many have sought to abase the creature too much, in effect placing sinners beyond the reach of a Savior. This does not honor him at all. Our need was truly desperate; apart from him we were completely lost. But when he saved, he *saved*. Too many in the Reformed tradition think that it honors God to live their lives in three accumulated feet of total depravity, and from time to time they go completely under.

Others, of the "happy, happy, happy all the day" school of

thought, have slight views of sin, and hence slight views of grace. Some think that sin is so great that grace can't deal with it. Others think that sin is so trivial that not very much grace is needed. Both disparage the greatness of the grace of God.

When Christ saves, he saves to the *uttermost*. He actually delivers us. He forgives us, and this makes a profound difference in how we respond to him, and in how we live our daily lives. One of the great differences his salvation brings is summed up in the word *joy*. We are obviously acquainted with the joy that our salvation should bring to us. In this portion of Hebrews, we see the joy which our salvation brings to *him*, and this is the real mind-bender.

> For he who sanctifies and those who are sanctified all have one source. That is why he is not ashamed to call them brothers, saying,
>
> "I will tell of your name to my brothers;
> in the midst of the congregation I will sing your praise."
>
> And again,
>
> "I will put my trust in him."
>
> And again,
>
> "Behold, I and the children God has given me." (Heb. 2:11–13)

In the previous verse of this chapter (v. 10), we learned that Christ is the prince, the captain of our salvation. He is the Lord of salvation, and hence the Lord of the saved. Now we should note carefully what the prince of salvation does here. He says something, and in that statement he identifies certain people as his brethren. Whom does he call brethren?

First, those who are under his authority are in the process of being *sanctified*. We know that our holiness here is not the ground of our salvation at all. No creature was ever put right with God through his own pitiful efforts, whether he lived in Rome or Geneva. At the same time, we know that where there is no holiness, there is no heaven. Without holiness, no one will see the Lord. Christ identifies his brethren as those who are being sanctified.

Secondly, we must note that this sanctification is not something we do "for God." Who is the one who sanctifies? *Christ* sanctifies. Who is being sanctified? The answer is those who are being led to salvation. We don't sanctify ourselves, in whole or in part, so that God will have something to do with us. God has something to do with us in Christ, and that something is sanctification.

Christ and his people are "all of one." We share in a common new humanity in Christ; we are *one people*. The one who sanctifies and those who are being sanctified are all one. Consequently, Christ is not ashamed to call us his brethren. He is not ashamed because the purpose of God is manifest throughout the process—even though the process is not yet complete. In our justification, we are completed. In our sanctification, we will be completed. In neither case is Christ ashamed. He is not ashamed of what he *has* done for us, and he is not ashamed of what he *will* do for us.

We learn later in Hebrews that Christ endured the cross, despising the shame of it, because of the joy that was set before him (Heb. 12:1–2). In this place, we learn that Christ sings praise to God in the midst of the congregation. We are gathered together as a great assembly, as a great congregation, and Christ is in the midst of us. From within our midst, *he* sings the praises of God. He is the singer, he is the soloist. How easy it is for us to forget that our God is full, everlastingly full, of *joy*.

This joy includes his joy over the salvation of creatures such as ourselves. In Luke 15, notice how Christ speaks of the finding of the lost sheep and the lost coin. "Just so, I tell you, there will be *more joy* in heaven *over one sinner* who repents than over ninety-nine righteous persons who need no repentance" (Luke 15:7). "Likewise, I say to you, there is *joy in the presence of the angels of God* over one sinner who repents" (Luke 15:10). Notice that this is not angels rejoicing. This is angels watching God rejoice. This is joy in the presence of the angels of God. We worship and serve a God who *delights* in saving his people. Of course the angels rejoice over repentance, just as we do, but this joy is derivative. We reflect this joy as the moon reflects sunlight. God is filled to overflowing with joy, and one of his reasons for joy is the state of the people he has forgiven.

In our zeal to protect the holiness and justice of God, we have in effect slandered him. No creature can approach the happiness of the triune God. "The LORD your God is in your midst, a mighty one who will save; *he will rejoice over you with gladness*; he will quiet you by his love; *he will exult over you with loud singing*" (Zeph. 3:17). God is glad, and God is joyful. Most Christians can deal with that, assuming it is an attributes-of-God thing. Note this, however. He rejoices over his people with gladness. He looks at your church, assembled as you were on Sunday, and he breaks into song. *That* is the weird part.

Our response must consequently not be mumbling our way through psalms and hymns. We have been saved by someone who does not do this. God through Christ wanted to save us, and rejoices in having done so. He is not at all sorry about it.

The three quotations from the Old Testament in this passage are all offered to make the same basic point. Christ, our Lord, is *one of us*. The quotations are from Psalm 22 and Isaiah 8 respectively. Consider Psalm 22. This exultation immediately follows the prophecy of the resurrection. And in Isaiah 8, the prophet is speaking of the cornerstone, which is also the rock of stumbling. We are his brothers, and so we do not stumble over him. By singing just as he sings, we show that we have not stumbled over him.

BILLIONS OF HIS BRETHREN

Christ is not ashamed to be our brother. He is not ashamed to share completely in our humanity. Further than this, he was not ashamed to be identified with us in our sin and folly. This is what he did throughout the course of his ministry. He began at the baptism of John by identifying completely with sinners; it was, after all, a baptism of repentance. This troubled John; Jesus did not need to repent. Through the course of his entire ministry, he identified with Israel. He was baptized, like Israel was in the cloud and sea. He went into the wilderness for forty days, just as Israel had for forty years. He was tempted there, just as Israel was. After the trial, he began his conquest of Canaan, just as Israel had. In Christ, we have the arrival of the new Israel, the new man, the new way of being human. His identification with us as sinners culminated in his death on the cross, and the new humanity was established in the resurrection. This is the message of the cross.

> Since therefore the children share in flesh and blood, he himself likewise partook of the same things, that through death he might destroy the one who has the power of death, that is, the devil, and deliver all those who through fear of death were subject to lifelong slavery. For surely it is not angels that he helps, but he helps the offspring of Abraham. Therefore he had to be made like his brothers in every respect, so that he might become a merciful and faithful high priest in the service of God, to make propitiation for the sins of the people. For because he himself has suffered when tempted, he is able to help those who are being tempted. (Heb. 2:14–18)

Christ is not ashamed of us as his brethren, but we as his "children" share flesh and blood. He likewise shared in this common humanity, in order to accomplish his final and ultimate purpose. That purpose was to release us from the bondage of death, and to do so through destroying the devil, who had the power of death. As it says, Christ does not offer this redemption to angels, but rather to the seed of Abraham. Consequently, he was made like us in order to represent us to God, and to make propitiation for our sins. Sharing in our humanity, being tempted, and suffering to the point of death, means that he is able to help us—we who are tempted now.

The Bible teaches us that the sting of death comes from the fact that we are sinners, and under the curse of God (1 Cor. 15:56). Prior to the cross, we are told that the devil had authority of some kind over death. This authority is probably from his relationship to sin. He is the accuser of the brethren; the devil is the prosecutor. He loves to bring charges; the devil loves arraignments. We are accustomed to think of the devil as ultimately foul, but the devil appears as an angel of light. He does not understand himself as the ultimate dirt, but he is the ultimate digger of dirt. Christ came in order to destroy him *in this office*. Christ came to bring forgiveness, to throw down the power of accusation.

We do not fear death because we die; we fear death because *we deserve to die*. When the devil accuses us, we know that he has a point. God told Adam that the day he ate from the fruit he would surely die. Ezekiel tells us that the soul that sins shall die. Paul tells us that the wages of sin are death. If we came innocent to an experience like death, the situation would be different, but we are not innocent, and this is why we are tempted to fear death.

This is why we must come to understand the greatness of the cross, which is directly related to the greatness of Christ. The apostle Paul said that he resolved to know nothing but Christ, and him crucified. Note that the one who died is an object of knowledge in the first place. Who is *he*? And having answered the question, the incarnate Word of God himself, we come to proclaim *him* crucified.

We are told here that Christ came in order to destroy the devil in his princedom over death. This conquering aspect of the cross is seen in the New Testament again and again. "Now is the judgment of this world; *now will the ruler of this world be cast out*. And I, when I am lifted up from the earth, will draw all people to myself" (John 12:31–32). What will Jesus do in his death? He will cast out the ruler of this world. What will Jesus do in his death? He will draw all peoples to himself. Why do I believe that through the preaching of the gospel, the kingdom of Christ will grow and expand until it fills the earth with the knowledge of the Lord, as the waters cover the sea? Why do I think this? For two reasons. Because Jesus died and consequently, one, the ruler of this world has been cast out, and two, all peoples are being drawn to Jesus. "This he set aside, nailing it to the cross. He disarmed the rulers and authorities and put them to open shame, by triumphing over them in him" (Col. 2:14–15). The cross was not just a defeat for the principalities and powers, *technically* speaking. It was a humiliating defeat; it was a rout. *Christus Victor*.

Remember that Christ stands in the middle of the great congregation; he is not ashamed to be with *us*, the children God has given him. In the cross, Christ was not attempting to save those angels who had fallen. He offered them no help. Rather, he was saving the seed of Abraham. He had to be made like us, his brethren, so that he could make propitiation for the sins of his people. Propitiation means the turning aside of wrath. From whom is this wrath turned aside? *His brethren.* For whom is propitiation made? And not for us only, but also for the sins of the whole world (1 John 2:1ff.). Put these two things together, and we see that the world will be saved, that the world will be filled with billions of his brethren, and that Jesus will sing in the midst of the great congregation indeed.

Christ was *our* high priest. That which was offered to God in the sacrifice of the cross was *a nature like ours*, only without sin. Remember this always: the priest who offered this sacrifice also had a nature like ours, yet without sin. Because our priest and our sacrifice understands temptation and understands the human frame, he is able to help you here, now, and in the day of your dying. Our older brother has gone through it already, and has graciously removed the sting of it.

6

Apostle and High Priest

In this next portion of Hebrews, we see a wonderful unity, where the writer ties together heaven and earth, Old Testament saints and New Testament saints, Christ and Moses.

> Therefore, holy brothers, you who share in a heavenly calling, consider Jesus, the apostle and high priest of our confession, who was faithful to him who appointed him, just as Moses also was faithful in all God's house. For Jesus has been counted worthy of more glory than Moses—as much more glory as the builder of a house has more honor than the house itself. (For every house is built by someone, but the builder of all things is God.) Now Moses was faithful in all God's house as a servant, to testify to the things that were to be spoken later, but Christ is faithful over God's house as a son. And we are his house if indeed we hold fast our confidence and our boasting in our hope. (Heb. 3:1–6)

So the brethren are holy because they are brethren together with him. As such, we should consider (again!) our Lord Jesus Christ. We should consider him in his offices of apostle and high priest. Returning to the comparison with Moses, our author tells us that both Christ and Moses were faithful "in the house." But Christ is still much greater because there are ranks within the household. Moses was a faithful servant in the house, looking forward to the time of the heir, while Christ was both the builder of the house, and Lord over it. What is this house? The house is the people of God—both at the time of Moses, and before, and at the time of Christ, and ever since. All believers inhabit the same house. Christians are Jews, and Moses is a Christian.

The phrase "apostle and high priest" is striking. This is the one place in Scripture where Christ is called an *apostle*, that is, one who is sent out. A "sent one" has the authority and commission of the one sending. For example, an apostle of a church is like a missionary or church planter. An apostle of Christ is sent out by Christ and has his authority, as did the Twelve. In this instance, Christ is described as an apostle. He was sent out by God the Father, and represents God to us. At the same time, he is also described as a high priest—that is, as one of *us* to represent us to God. A priest is chosen from among the people and stands before them to represent them. This phrase "apostle and high priest" therefore means that Christ is the perfect bridge between God and man. As an apostle of God, he represents God perfectly to us, and as our high priest, he represents us perfectly to God.

Just as the author was at pains to show Christ's supremacy over the angels, so he needed to show Christ's supremacy over Moses. This was not because he had a disparaging view of angels or Moses, but rather because he was writing to a group of Christians in danger of going back to the old shadows of Judaism. In that Judaism, inflated views of angels and Moses were common. So he continues the contrast between Moses and Christ, but not to make the point that they were on opposite sides. Such a false dichotomy existed in the minds of the apostates who fell away, but such opposition is not found in Scripture. Moses and Christ were not distinct because they were enemies; they were distinct because Christ was lord of the house, and Moses was a servant in the house. The distinction was *hierarchical*. They were alike in faithfulness, and distinct in rank.

In addition to this, the author of Hebrews shows that not only was Christ greater as Lord of the house, he was also greater as the builder of the house. And the house that he built was composed of people—including Moses.

We are that house. The Bible is very clear that *we* are God's building, God's house. As well as constituting the structure, we are also the inhabitants. For example: "Do you not know that you are God's temple and that God's Spirit dwells in you? If anyone destroys God's temple, God will destroy him. For God's temple is holy, and you are that temple" (1 Cor. 3:16–17). "As you come to him, a living stone rejected by men but in the sight of God chosen and precious, you yourselves like living stones are being built up as a spiritual house, to be a holy priesthood, to offer spiritual sacrifices acceptable to God through Jesus Christ" (1 Pet. 2:4–5).

Given this, what is necessary? We must hold firm to the end. We see here, stated plainly, the doctrine of perseverance. Whose house we are, *if* . . . three classes of men exist. Some are never in the house. They have no connection to the Christian faith at all. Some are in the house, but only temporarily. They are covenantally connected to Christ, and the connection is a real one, but they are not elect. The true sons of the house, however, the elect of God, abide there forever. "The slave does not remain in the house forever; the son remains forever. So if the Son sets you free, you will be free indeed" (John 8:35–36).

AN EVIL HEART OF UNBELIEF

As we consider the remainder of the third chapter of Hebrews, we must remember what we have already learned about the house of Christ. He is the lord over *the same house* in which Moses served. We see the importance of understanding this as we consider the duty of repentance under the New Covenant.

Therefore, as the Holy Spirit says,
"Today, if you hear his voice,
do not harden your hearts as in the rebellion,
on the day of testing in the wilderness,
where your fathers put me to the test
and saw my works for forty years.
Therefore I was provoked with that generation,
and said, 'They always go astray in their heart;
they have not known my ways.'
As I swore in my wrath,
'They shall not enter my rest.' "

Take care, brothers, lest there be in any of you an evil, unbelieving heart, leading you to fall away from the living God. But exhort one another every day, as long as it is called "today," that none of you may be hardened by the deceitfulness of sin. For we have come to share in Christ, if indeed we hold our original confidence firm to the end. As it is said,

"Today, if you hear his voice,
do not harden your hearts as in the rebellion."

For who were those who heard and yet rebelled? Was it not all those who left Egypt led by Moses? And with whom was he provoked for forty years? Was it not with those who sinned, whose bodies fell in the wilderness? And to whom did he swear that they would not enter his rest, but to those who were disobedient? So we see that they were unable to enter because of unbelief. (Heb. 3:7–19)

The author of Hebrews quotes here from Psalm 95. The theme of the psalm is clearly salvation (v. 1), and clear, humble worship (vv. 6–7). When the Lord's voice speaks, and a man hears it, and the day can be called *today*, then he has a moral duty to not harden his heart. The one addressed should not sin in the same way that *his fathers* sinned. A very common temptation confronts Reformed Christians who are influenced by the prevailing baptistic assumptions around us. This temptation is to draw *contrasts* between us and the Jews in the wilderness at precisely the points where the New Testament draws *parallels*.

The author of Hebrews is saying that we need to listen in just the same way that they needed to listen. We need to guard against hardness of heart in just the same way that they needed to guard against hardness of heart. Brethren, he says, take care that an evil heart of unbelief not be found in any of you. Any of you what? Any of you *brethren*.

So the writer is saying, "Brethren, beware." This is the larger purpose of the entire epistle. The words of the psalm are applied to these first-century believers. The speaker addresses them as his brethren, which means they are also brethren to Christ, and to Moses . . . and to those who fell in the wilderness. This means that scriptural warnings based upon what happened to the Jews in the wilderness are applicable within the New Covenant. Moreover, they will be applicable as long as any man can say, "Today."

Apostasy is a real sin, committed by real people. This is something that Arminians get, and that most Calvinists do not get. To be sure, not one of the elect can ever be taken out of God's electing and sovereign decree. This is something that Calvinists get, and that Arminians do not get. Arminians can read Romans 8–11 and not see the absolute sovereignty of God, which is something that never ceases to astonish me. Still, lest we Calvinists get on a high horse, Arminians can read though Hebrews and see real apostasy there. Few things are more exegetically embarrassing than to hear a Calvinist talk about how the warnings are hypothetical, like "keep off the grass" signs in the middle of the Sahara. Many things can be said to this, but the most compelling is that the warnings invariably deny that they are the least bit hypothetical. Like here: "Do not harden your hearts as in the rebellion." The rebellion referred to was not hypothetical, and neither was the warning to not do it again.

We are talking about the sin of unbelief. The sin warned against here is that of *evil unbelief*, pure and simple. Not only is it unbelief, it is unbelief resulting in *apostasy*—departure from the living God, falling away from the living God. The sin is spoken of in the sternest possible way—rebellion, hardened hearts, evil heart of unbelief, and a departure from God. Now, in order to *depart* from the living God, a man has to have been in some measure, in some way, connected to the living God. Can he depart from the ultimate decrees, made before the foundation of the world? Of course not—that would be nonsensical. But can he fall away from a real, covenantal union with Christ, a union that exists objectively here in this world? Absolutely, and that is what this epistle is seeking to prevent.

These warnings are addressed to those who have been partakers of Christ. The word *partaker* is important in the book of Hebrews. They are addressed as *partakers* of the heavenly calling (3:1). *Partakers* of the Holy Spirit cannot be brought to repentance if they fall away (6:4). All legitimate sons are *partakers* of God's chastening (12:8). And here, those who hold their confidence firm to the end are genuine *partakers* of Christ.

So who falls away? The warning in verse 12 is to those who would be tempted by their evil heart of unbelief to *depart* from the living God. One cannot depart from a place where he isn't. Who was it who fell in the wilderness? Were they not those who had been led out from Egypt by Moses?

We see the warnings are directed against those who were in covenant with God, but who fell into unbelief. This book is about the sin of apostasy. Can a Christian fall away? Yes. Can someone who is truly regenerate, elect of God, an eternal Christian, fall away? No, clearly not. This means that unbelievers *within the covenant* receive a stricter judgment. The Bible teaches us that men are divided into three important classes—unbelievers outside the covenant, unbelievers within the covenant, and believers within the covenant. At the last day, there will only be two categories, but until that day, as long as it is called *today*, the three categories are still being sorted into two categories.

Those in this second category fell in the wilderness many years ago. So shall we, if we do not *believe*. If we are the elect of God, we will persevere in that evangelical belief. If we are not, then we will not. In either case, we are in the covenanted household of Christ unless and until we depart from it.

THINGS THAT ACCOMPANY SALVATION

One of the perennial pastoral problems in the church is the question of assurance of salvation. On the one hand, some Christians hold that to seek *any* kind of solid assurance is presumptuous. On the other hand are those Christians who appear to glory in just that kind of presumption—"Just pray this prayer, and *wham*, you're in forever." There is a third way—full assurance and no presumption. "I write these things to you who believe in the name of the Son of God that *you may know* that you have eternal life" (1 John 5:13).

> And with whom was he provoked for forty years? Was it not with those who sinned, whose bodies fell in the wilderness? And to whom did he swear that they would not enter his rest, but to those who were disobedient? So we see that they were unable to enter because of unbelief.
>
> Therefore, while the promise of entering his rest still stands, let us fear lest any of you should seem to have failed to reach it. For good news came to us just as to them, but the message they heard did not benefit them, because they were not united by faith with those who listened. For we who have believed enter that rest, as he has said. (Heb. 3:17–4:3a)

The writer to the Hebrews is confronting a very real pastoral crisis. A number of the Christians he knows are contemplating apostasy—abandoning the Christian faith, and returning to the types and shadows of the Old Covenant, the blood of bulls and goats. If they left the faith, that would be a real apostasy. Would it be a fall from the eternal determinations of God? Of course not. But would it be a fall from *something*? Yes, of course. As the author of Hebrews considers this problem, his mind turns to a parallel situation in the Old Testament, the time the people of Israel spent in the wilderness, and how many of them fell away from God there. He takes this theme from Psalm 95. With whom was God grieved for forty years? With those he had delivered from Egypt, but who sinned and whose bodies fell in the wilderness (3:17). God, speaking to the people he had delivered, swore that some would never enter his rest. Who made up that group? Those *that did not believe* (3:18). The thing that shut them out was their unbelief (3:19). So then, he says, turning to these first-century Christians, let us fear lest any of us fall short of the rest. Not everyone who is set aside *by* the gospel is set aside *in* the gospel (4:2). When the word is preached, mix it with your faith (4:2). Those who *believe* are always those who enter the rest of God (4:3). *Sola fide.*

You can't lose what you never had. We need to understand this basic principle at the first. You can never lose what you never had. This means if someone maintains he can never lose his salvation, even though he lives like the devil, and this "unloseable" salvation is his because he "prayed a prayer once," he is resting in a false confidence. This man cannot lose his salvation for the same reason that I cannot lose my Argentinian citizenship. He doesn't have it to begin with.

This illustrates the difference between the very popular "once saved, always saved" doctrine and the Reformed doctrine of the perseverance of the saints. Now it is *true* that if someone is *truly* saved, then that person is always saved. How can we tell? We can tell if they persevere in faith and holiness to the end.

We have to be very careful here because saving faith always looks to Christ and his promises. Saving faith does not focus on the presence or absence of saving faith. We are supposed to be looking to Jesus, the author and finisher of our faith. We are not to be looking at ourselves, trying to determine if we are believing or not. "Myself believing" is not the proper object of my faith. Christ is the object of our faith. As we believe Christ and his promises, we will certainly be (dimly) aware that we are doing so, but we should never get distracted by that.

That said . . . the Bible *does* say that it is appropriate under certain circumstances to examine yourself (2 Cor. 13: 5). You must examine yourself using *biblical* criteria, and not your own made-up standards, like "maybe I don't love Jesus enough." Here are the biblical standards. *You are looking to Jesus Christ in faith, and you confess him* (Romans 10:9; 1 John 4:15; "Whoever confesses that Jesus is the Son of God, God abides in him, and he in God"). *God has given you the gift of his Spirit* (1 John 4:13; "By this we know that we abide in him and he in us, because he has given us of his Spirit"). *We love other Christians* (1 John 3:14; "We know that we have passed out of death into life, because we love the brothers. Whoever does not love abides in death"). *We have been given humility of mind* (Matthew 18:3; "Unless you turn and become like children, you will never enter the kingdom of heaven"). *A true Christian understands spiritual things* (1 Corinthians 1:18; "For the word of the cross is folly to those who are perishing, but to us who are being saved it is the power of God"). *The natural man doesn't get it* (1 Corinthians 2:14). *Christians obey God* (1 John 2:3; "And by this we know that we have come to know him, if we keep his commandments"). *Christians disobey God, and* catch *it* (Hebrews 12:5–8; ". . . For the Lord disciplines the one he loves. . . .").

Remember, you only look at these things with your peripheral vision—straight on, you are looking to Christ.

Always remember the difference between a doubt and a question. A doubt is something that cannot ever be answered in principle. It starts off with, what if *this*? The reply should be, what if *that*? "What if Jesus isn't divine?" is a doubt. "What does Paul teach on the deity and humanity of Christ?" is a question. "What if my husband isn't faithful?" is a doubt. What if he is? "Who is that blonde in the red convertible driving around town with him?" is a question, and actually, as questions go, it is a pretty good one.

Keep it simple. You have no right to *doubt* your salvation. Look to Christ. And if you find all kinds of indications that you have never looked to Christ, then that should give rise to some honest *questions*. The early Christians ate and drank together in gladness and simplicity of heart. Don't over-engineer it. As Martin Luther put it once—do you doubt whether you are elected to salvation? "Then say your prayers, man, and you may conclude that you are. It is as easy as that."

7

A New Testament Deuteronomy

God loves a cheerful giver. Those who work frantically in his presence displease him. Those who believe, those who enter rest, are equipped for evangelical work—refreshed work.

> Therefore, while the promise of entering his rest still stands, let us fear lest any of you should seem to have failed to reach it. For good news came to us just as to them, but the message they heard did not benefit them, because they were not united by faith with those who listened. For we who have believed enter that rest, as he has said,
>
> > "As I swore in my wrath,
> > 'They shall not enter my rest,' "

> although his works were finished from the foundation of the world. For he has somewhere spoken of the seventh day in this way: "And God rested on the seventh day from all his works." And again in this passage he said,
>
> "They shall not enter my rest."
>
> Since therefore it remains for some to enter it, and those who formerly received the good news failed to enter because of disobedience, again he appoints a certain day, "Today," saying through David so long afterward, in the words already quoted,
>
> "Today, if you hear his voice,
> do not harden your hearts."
>
> For if Joshua had given them rest, God would not have spoken of another day later on. So then, there remains a Sabbath rest for the people of God, for whoever has entered God's rest has also rested from his works as God did from his.
>
> Let us therefore strive to enter that rest, so that no one may fall by the same sort of disobedience. For the word of God is living and active, sharper than any two-edged sword, piercing to the division of soul and of spirit, of joints and of marrow, and discerning the thoughts and intentions of the heart. And no creature is hidden from his sight, but all are naked and exposed to the eyes of him to whom we must give account.
>
> Since then we have a great high priest who has passed through the heavens, Jesus, the Son of God, let us hold fast our confession. (Heb. 4:1–14)

A promise of salvation rest exists as long as it can be called "*today*." The professing Christians of the first century were in a very similar situation as the Jews in the wilderness were. Both had heard the gospel, and *in both cases* some of God's covenant people heard with faith and some did not. In both cases, those who had believed entered God's rest—exclusion from the rest being the threat given in the psalm. Even though God has rested from creation since the sixth day, some through lack of faith do not *enter* that rest. The initial sabbath rest at creation and the Canaan rest spoken of in Scripture did not exhaust the promise. In effect, they *were* the promise. The promise extends down throughout all history—whenever there is a *today*. The rest which we enter by faith is salvation rest. Christ rested from his work of the new creation just as God rested from his work of creation. However, neither profits apart from faith. We must work hard, be diligent, to enter rest, and remember that God sees the heart.

The Jews in the wilderness and the Christians in the first century were parallel peoples. Remember that our author is not *contrasting* the Jews and Christians—he *compares* them to one another. They had the gospel preached to them, just as we have (v. 2). The Christians of the first century who were contemplating a return to the sacrifices of "bulls and goats" were in the same position as those Jews who wanted to return to Egypt. The New Testament draws a broad typological parallel between the history of the Jews in the Old Testament and the people of God in the New. The captivity in Egypt is parallel to the entire Old Covenant era. God brought them all out of the land of Egypt, and they spent forty years in the wilderness. The church was brought out of her captivity in the resurrection of Jesus, and spent the next forty years in the wilderness. Jesus rose from the dead around 30 AD and that forty-year period ended in 70 AD. During *that* forty years, the church went through her wilderness testing—receiving the word of God, establishing apostolic authority, and so on. And then in 70 AD the "invasion of Canaan" began, where the world is now Canaan, and the exploits of the new Joshua are subduing all nations under his feet.

This makes the book of Hebrews a New Testament Deuteronomy, given to the people of God at the end of their forty-year period, and given as a preparation for how they were going to conduct themselves in the land that the Lord their God was giving to them.

After his conquest of sin and death, the Lord Jesus established a new creation. He was the agent of this second creation, just as he was the agent of the first. In this passage, we see Christ resting. Just as God created all things, and then rested, so Christ re-created all things, and then rested. After each work was complete, the rest was ongoing, but living in the midst of that ongoing rest was of no value to those who did not mix this understanding with faith. Consequently, the people of God have the first day on which to worship just as the Jews had the seventh day. The day is not the center—Christ is the center. In other words, God created the heavens and earth in six days and then rested. Christ re-created the heavens and earth, making a new heavens and earth, and then rested. He did this in three days and nights—half the time. When he emerged from the grave on the first day of the week, he was entering his resurrection rest. This is why a "sabbath rest" remains for the people of God.

This is also the central reason why Christians do not observe the seventh day as their day of rest. Given the "everlasting" language of the Old Testament with regard to the sabbath, nothing short of a *new creation* could have moved that day from the seventh to the first. The seventh day was imbedded in the created order, and it would stay that way until the created order was overhauled, redone, re-created—which it was in the resurrection of Jesus.

Jesus's resurrection is the basis of all covenant obedience. We see here, as we see all through Hebrews, the ongoing fact of blessing and curses. This is the nature of covenants. We are to be diligent to enter the rest. Note the cooperative contrast between *diligence* and *resting*. We are to rest in the presence of a two-edged sword, which can slice us as thinly as possible. He discerns the thoughts and intentions of the heart. No creature is out of his view, and we must all give an account to him. *This* is the foundation of *rest*?!

Yes—God deals with his people by means of covenant. Consequently, when we live under him in a covenantal fashion we are living in the way he made us to live. This does not "work" because it makes sense to us; it *works* because this is how God made the world.

SALVATION REST

We see in the first two chapters of Genesis that the coming gospel is pictured in *three* distinct ways. The first is marriage (Eph. 5:32), and the second is the creation of light, which is alluded to in 2 Corinthians 4:6. The last is our subject here—the *rest* God took at the completion of his creation. "And on the seventh day God finished his work that he had done, and he rested on the seventh day from all his work that he had done" (Gen. 2:2).

That passage from Genesis is quoted in Hebrews 4:4—"For he has somewhere spoken of the seventh day in this way: 'And God rested on the seventh day from all his works.' " This passage is quoted by the author of Hebrews in the midst of a detailed argument on the nature of *salvation by rest*. This is how the argument is presented.

What day is it? In Hebrews 3:7, the writer cites Psalm 95. "*Today*, if you hear his voice, do not harden your hearts as in the rebellion. . . ." A little later (v. 11), he speaks of those who did harden their hearts. "As I swore in my wrath, 'They shall not enter *my rest*.' " The rest here is typified by the land of Canaan. They did not enter Canaan-rest because of their unbelief.

When is this warning valid? As long as there are days called *today*. That is, as long as history has not come to an end, men should hear and heed his voice. How is the warning to be heeded? Through faith and only through faith. Look at the repetition.

3:12—evil, *unbelieving* heart
3:14—if . . . we hold . . . our original *confidence* firm to the end
3:19—they were unable to enter because of *unbelief*
4:2—did not benefit them, because they were not united by *faith*
4:3—we who have *believed* do enter that rest

Now some might want to see the same critique of unbelief in 4:10.

4:10—For whoever has entered God's rest has also *rested from his works* as God did from his.

However, as argued here, the reference is to Christ resting from his work of re-creation just as God rested from his work of creation. Otherwise, the comparison is somewhat odd. Did God rest in the same way we do after we quit trying to save ourselves in our pride and arrogance?

Now consider how the writer integrates his quotations from the Old Testament into his argument. "For we who have believed enter that rest, as he has said, 'As I swore in my wrath, "They shall not enter my rest," ' although his works were finished from the foundation of the world. For he has somewhere spoken of the seventh day in this way: 'And God rested on the seventh day from all his works.' And again in this passage he said, 'They shall not enter my rest.' " (Heb. 4:3–5). The rest typified by Canaan is the same rest which is typified by the first Sabbath. What does it all mean? *Salvation is not through striving*. Nor is it through *our* resting. Salvation is through *God's* work and rest. He says, "They shall not enter m*y* rest."

Faith is not doing; faith is resting. This is hard for us to grasp. It must therefore be grasped *for* us. Consider verse 11. "Let us therefore *strive* to enter that *rest*, so that no one may fall by the same sort of disobedience." Unless the grace of God is at work within us, it cannot be done. We are sinners who want to have our own righteousness. Unless it is given to us, we will die without it.

Crushed Boldness

As we live out our Christian lives, we must always remember that this is not something we do detached from God, for God. Rather, we are to live our lives in Christ, and on the basis of what he has done for us. Our central interest is therefore the gospel, and the great truths of the gospel. They are to be our food and nourishment.

> Since then we have a great high priest who has passed through the heavens, Jesus, the Son of God, let us hold fast our confession. For we do not have a high priest who is unable to sympathize with our weaknesses, but one who in every respect has been tempted as we are, yet without sin. Let us then with confidence draw near to the throne of grace, that we may receive mercy and find grace to help in time of need. (Heb. 4:14–16)

We have already seen that we must persevere to the end. The Jews who fell in the wilderness did not do so. But nevertheless *our* perseverance is not based upon *our* performance. The recipients of this letter are urged to hold fast their confession *because of* what Jesus has done, and because of the office he holds. As we resist the temptations which would turn us aside from the way, we must remember that we have a sympathetic high priest—one who, without sin, knows what temptation is like. On the basis of this, we are told to come before the throne of grace boldly in order to receive forgiveness for our failures and strength for our trials.

This is what it means to hold fast. When we see Jesus, we hold fast. When we try to look at *how* we are holding fast, we do not hold fast. We cannot hold fast by looking at our fingers; we must look at him. We are urged throughout this epistle to see Jesus, to consider Jesus. When we meditate on his person and work, his nature and attributes, we are strengthened to hold fast. When we concentrate on "holding fast" we lose our grip and slip away. We are to have faith in Christ, not faith in our faith. We are to hold to him, not hold to our holding.

We are told here to hold fast our *confession*. The object of our faith as Christians is objective and outside ourselves. We do not confess the condition of our hearts; we confess the truth outside our hearts. Because God has been gracious enough to cleanse our hearts, and to show us their true condition, we confess the truth gladly and with a whole heart. We are saved by looking *away*, and never by looking *in*. So look away to the truth, and hold fast.

How are we to live, tempted as we are? Many things distract us from our duty of faithful confession. The world is a sinful and complicated place. How can we maneuver our way to heaven? The answer given here is that we do not have to figure it out on our own. Christ has gone on before us—and not just from earth to heaven. He has gone from a condition of temptation and turmoil, just like ours in every respect, to a condition in glory free from the very presence of sin. The only place he differs from us is found in the fact that he has never sinned. But this is not a "deficiency" in his ability to be sympathetic. The fact that he never sinned means that he understands sin *better* than we do, and he has fully experienced the force of temptation. If a group of ten men were walking along in 70 MPH winds, and nine of them blew over right away, and the tenth walked all the way home, which one knows the most about wind? The Lord Jesus knows far more about temptation and sin than we do. We blow over in temptation right away, and then, lying on the ground, we make ourselves out to be wind experts. By the grace of God, repentance from sin can be instructive, but falling into sin never is.

We are summoned, therefore, to have a crushed boldness. The result of all this is an obligation—we must come before the throne of *grace* with *boldness*. Those Christians who neglect the teaching of this epistle fall over on one side or the other. They either crawl and grovel before God because they are such miserable sinners—implying that the blood of Christ cleaned them up inadequately—or they breeze into the throne room of God (in sweats and flip-flops) because they assume they were not all that bad off to begin with. The biblical balance is found by the sinner who has begun to understand the gravity and greatness of his sin, but, through the grace of God, has been given a glimpse of the greatness of his Savior. Remember that we are to approach God, seeing that we have such a *great* high priest. Our sin is great, but our high priest is greater. There is no way to minimize the nature of our sin without minimizing the office of the Lord Jesus.

When we come before the throne of God in this fashion, we receive *mercy* for our sins. As you grow in your Christian walk, do not expect your awareness of your sinfulness to diminish. It will only diminish if you are hardening your heart and lying to yourself. God was very kind to Paul—he grew in grace so much that by the *end* of his life he was the "chief of sinners." Go thou and do likewise.

The other side of the coin is equally important. We receive grace to help us in time of need. If our lives are not truly, objectively changing, by the grace of Christ, it is a bad sign indeed. If we are not growing in practical holiness, we will not see the Lord.

8

Maturity and Discernment

In this next chapter of Hebrews, we begin a short introduction to the nature of Christ's priesthood and intercession for us. The writer of Hebrews is then diverted into a discussion of immaturity and apostasy before he returns to this theme in the middle chapters of his book.

> For every high priest chosen from among men is appointed to act on behalf of men in relation to God, to offer gifts and sacrifices for sins. He can deal gently with the ignorant and wayward, since he himself is beset with weakness. Because of this he is obligated to offer sacrifice for his own sins just as he does for those of the people. And no one takes this honor for himself, but only when called by God, just as Aaron was.

> So also Christ did not exalt himself to be made a high priest,
> but was appointed by him who said to him,
>
> "You are my Son,
> today I have begotten you";
>
> as he says also in another place,
>
> "You are a priest forever,
> after the order of Melchizedek."
>
> In the days of his flesh, Jesus offered up prayers and supplications, with loud cries and tears, to him who was able to save him from death, and he was heard because of his reverence. Although he was a son, he learned obedience through what he suffered. And being made perfect, he became the source of eternal salvation to all who obey him, being designated by God a high priest after the order of Melchizedek.
>
> About this we have much to say, and it is hard to explain, since you have become dull of hearing. For though by this time you ought to be teachers, you need someone to teach you again the basic principles of the oracles of God. You need milk, not solid food, for everyone who lives on milk is unskilled in the word of righteousness, since he is a child. But solid food is for the mature, for those who have their powers of discernment trained by constant practice to distinguish good from evil. (Heb. 5:1–14)

We have already been shown that Christ is a sympathetic high priest. The necessity that he be sympathetic may be gathered from the fact that he is a priest at all. Sympathetic representation is part of the job description. The first four verses of this chapter show that compassionate intercession comes with the priesthood. But the earthly Aaronic priests offered sacrifices, not only for the sins of the people, but also for their own sins. In this respect, Christ was unlike the priests of the line of Aaron. Christ as a priest was a true priest, but he was much greater than the priests of the Mosaic law. But this did not make him less sympathetic; it did not make him less of a priest. Quite the reverse.

And just as the priests of Aaron did not assign the honor of priesthood to themselves, so Christ did not appoint himself to become our priest. In Psalm 2, God's statement that he had begotten Christ is assigned in this place to the priestly work of Christ. Further, in Psalm 110, God declares emphatically that Christ is a priest in the order of Melchizedek. The appointment came from God himself. This quotation of the second psalm ("Today I have begotten you. . . .") should also be set alongside the quotation of it in Acts 13, where that verse is applied to the resurrection. Putting the two together, we can see that in the resurrection, Christ was entering into his priestly office, passing from the one who was the sacrificial lamb to the priest who offers up that lamb in the holiest place in the heavenlies. This passage from Psalm 2 is talking about Christ being begotten from the dead, and as an ever-living priest, he enters into the priesthood of Melchizedek, who is without beginning of days or end of life.

The Aaronic priests offered sacrifices, first for themselves, and secondly for the people. Their sacrifices for themselves were for sin. Christ prayed for himself first as well, but he did not have to do this because of sin. Nevertheless, he still fits the pattern of a priest.

Christ entered into his perfection—not from a previous condition of *imperfection*, but from a condition of probationary or untested perfection. Thus it says that he "learned obedience" through his sufferings and he, "having been perfected," became the author of our salvation.

The goal and direction of Christian living is maturity. The longing for the "way it was when we were first converted" can be a subtle snare. If we are referring to our first love, then well and good. But too often it means that we long for the days before everything was so *complicated*. This kind of doctrinal infantilism pervades the church today and is to be soundly rejected. The author of Hebrews rebukes his readers for being dull when they should be sharp (v. 11); he rebukes them for not being able to teach (v. 12); he rebukes them for needing to be taught the basics (v. 12); and he rebukes them for needing milk, not solid food (v. 12). Those in this condition are babies, and, he says, unskilled in the word of righteousness. In contrast to this, those who partake of solid food are mature. Through long practice and reason of use, they are able to see and understand subtle distinctions between good and evil.

We should take careful note of what he means by maturity. Mature believers would be able to discuss the priesthood of the Lord. Those who are unskilled have to be taught the "first principles of the oracles of God" all over again. These first principles are identified a few verses later, at the first part of chapter six. They are the doctrines of repentance and faith, baptisms, laying on of hands, and the resurrection and subsequent judgment. These are defined for us here as *milk*. The doctrine of the priestly intercessory work of Christ as our high priest is identified as solid food. Notice that certain ethical distinctions require maturity, experience, and long practice in order for us to be able to make them. Ethical distinctions (of a certain kind) are not equally obvious to everyone. All men know that it is wrong to kill your grandmother for her money. But what does it take to see the sins of worldliness? Or flattery? Or other subtle sins? Legalism arises when Christian communities try to have the fruit of discernment (the ability to make fine distinctions) without having the maturity that is necessary.

How long have you been a Christian? Do these admonitions apply to you? What is your condition of maturity? Do you need someone to go over the basics with you again? Or are you diligently applying the basics, and are hungry for more? Further, if you are hungry for more, is the moral component at the center of it? Do you study the priesthood of Christ, for example, in order to discern both *good* and *evil*? Or are you functioning as some kind of a doctrine computer? In Scripture, doctrine is practical and high doctrine is highly practical. Those who disparage doctrine for the sake of practice are impractical. Those who disparage practice for the sake of doctrine are unskilled in the word of righteousness. We are *never* to put apart what God has joined together.

9

Baptism and Covenant Life

Baptism in water can be a complicated subject—and yet the author of Hebrews treats it as one of the Christian "basics." This should make us wary because the evangelical Christian world doesn't have this sorted out yet, and so it should also make us eager to sort it out—to grow up into maturity as our text is urging.

> Therefore let us leave the elementary doctrine of Christ and go on to maturity, not laying again a foundation of repentance from dead works and of faith toward God, and of instruction about washings, the laying on of hands, the resurrection of the dead, and eternal judgment. And this we will do if God permits. (Heb. 6:1–3)

The various particular doctrines mentioned here are repentance from dead work (v. 1), faith in God (v. 1), baptisms and washings (v. 2), laying on of hands (v. 2), resurrection of the dead (v. 2), and eternal judgment (v. 2). These are the particulars, but what is the general heading for all these? He describes them as "the elementary doctrine of *Christ*" (v. 1). We are talking about the basics, the integration point, the beginning, the foundation. The writer wants to get past this, which he will do, God willing (v. 3). We too should get past it, which is not the same thing as outgrowing it—you don't ever outgrow the root, but rather you grow *on* the root.

The point here is not so much to emphasize where paedobaptists and credobaptists differ, but rather to emphasize something that may result in surprising agreement—a shared understanding of the *covenant* meaning of baptism. When this is understood, it is a key that unlocks many difficult passages in the book of Hebrews. Our text is right at the beginning of the sixth chapter, a chapter famous for giving heartburn to Calvinists. If God has decreed (before the foundation of the world) that a person is going to be saved, then what on earth can "falling away" (v. 6) possibly refer to?

There is a two-fold connection to Christ. In this fallen world, the church will always struggle with the tension between true and false profession of faith in Christ. That is because, until the resurrection, it will always be possible to talk one way and live another. This is a dilemma that surfaced in the first generation of the church and has been present with us ever since. This is what happens when the first and second items on the list of "basics" are missing, but baptism, third on the list, is not missing. *Now* what?

Baptism in water is a covenant bond, and, as such, it can easily be compared to putting on the wedding ring in a wedding ceremony. Now nobody thinks that the metals of gold and silver have magic transformative powers—mystically changing the couple in the ceremony into husband and wife. Intention is important, which is why a wedding ceremony on a movie set doesn't do anything of the kind, even if all the words are said. In the same way, a baptism performed on a movie set doesn't accomplish anything. Yet, at the same time, the ritual of placing water on someone in the name of the Father, Son, and Holy Spirit is not "just water." The ritual transforms, but not by any kind of magic. The ritual transforms a person's status because *that is what rituals do.*

We believe that when someone has been baptized in this way, that person is covenantally bound to God. He is *obligated.* Obligated to do what? To fulfill the terms of the New Covenant, which is to repent of his sins and to believe in Jesus. Nothing more, and nothing less, and even that is a gift of God, lest any man should boast.

Instead of being confused by baptism, we should learn to see it as one of the great illuminating features of our lives. Now . . . let's use an illustration, where I trust we will all have no problem grasping the distinctions. Suppose a husband is unfaithful to his wife, chronically and flagrantly. Now, is he a "true" husband? The answer, easily, is yes and no. *Yes,* he is a true husband—the papers are filed at the county courthouse, and the vows were said in the presence of God and witnesses. *No,* he is not a true husband because you can't be a true husband unless you are a true *man.* This is an easy distinction for us to grasp.

Now if he confessed his adulteries to his wife, seeking her forgiveness, and she extended it, and said, "Finally, tonight you have become my husband," what would we think if he responded with, "Really? That means I wasn't your husband before, which means I wasn't really committing adultery. Cool." To play with words that way would be evidence he was not really repentant. He was a true husband, and greatly to be condemned because he was an untrue husband. And no, this is not a contradiction.

Now another man is baptized, but he lives like the devil and always has. Is he a true Christian? In the same way, yes and no. *Yes,* you were there when he was baptized. Of course he is a Christian. *No,* he is untrue to the truth of the gospel and has an unconverted and rotten heart.

Some Christians do not feel comfortable applying a sign of this significance to infants. Others of us are just fine with that. But where we agree is in the propriety of calling all baptized individuals to their covenant obligations to trust in Jesus alone for their salvation—and to treat those who will not do so as "adulterers," and not just "fornicators."

This helps us make sense of some of the exhortations found in the rest of the book of Hebrews. "How much worse punishment, do you think, will be deserved by the one who has spurned the Son of God, and has profaned the blood of the covenant by which he was sanctified, and has outraged the Spirit of grace?" (Heb. 10:29). "For it is impossible, in the case of those who have once been enlightened, who have tasted the heavenly gift, and have shared in the Holy Spirit . . . and then have fallen away, to restore them again to repentance" (Heb. 6:4, 6). "Therefore, while the promise of entering his rest still stands, let us fear lest any of you should seem to have failed to reach it" (Heb. 4:1). In short, connection to Christ *today* is not an "all or nothing" affair. It will be one way or the other at the last day, of course, but today if you hear his voice, do not harden your heart.

SUZY AT THE LAST TRUMP

The Bible is very clear that we cannot misplace, or lose, our salvation—as though our salvation were a possession of *ours*, like a set of car keys or something. Our salvation is not something we can lose, as though we owned it. Rather, Christ owns us. We have been purchased by Christ, and he owns us. Knowing that this is the case, and having full confidence in the comforting doctrines of eternal election, what do we do with passages like, well . . . Hebrews 6? There it is, in the Bible, big as life.

> Therefore let us leave the elementary doctrine of Christ and go on to maturity, not laying again a foundation of repentance from dead works and of faith toward God, and of instruction about washings, the laying on of hands, the resurrection of the dead, and eternal judgment. And this we will do if God permits. For it is impossible, in the case of those who have once been enlightened, who have tasted the heavenly gift, and have shared in the Holy Spirit, and have tasted the goodness of the word of God and the powers of the age to come, and then have fallen away, to restore them again to repentance, since they are crucifying once again the Son of God to their own harm and holding him up to contempt. For land that has drunk the rain that often falls on it,

> and produces a crop useful to those for whose sake it is cultivated, receives a blessing from God. But if it bears thorns and thistles, it is worthless and near to being cursed, and its end is to be burned.
>
> Though we speak in this way, yet in your case, beloved, we feel sure of better things—things that belong to salvation. (Heb. 6:1–9)

The author of Hebrews wants to press on beyond basic Christian doctrine. He does not want to abandon this foundation, but he does want to build on it. That foundation is repentance from religion, faith in God, the meaning of the Levitical washings or baptisms in the Law, the laying on of hands, the resurrection, and eternal judgment. He is not content with his readers remaining in an infantile state—he intends to press on. This is important because remaining in the foundational doctrines without pressing on creates the temptation toward apostasy. Those who have been initiated, who have tasted, but who do not press on to know Christ further, are in grave danger. Sticking with the basics only is therefore not a good way to stick to the basics.

This is the central problem with pietistic fundamentalism; at the end of the day it is counterproductive and does not defend the things it seeks to defend. The real way to "defend" a foundation is by *building* on it.

As we come to this passage, we must remember what we have learned throughout the rest of Scripture. First, this passage does *not* teach that one of the decreed elect can fall from their election. This would make sovereign election meaningless. This would in effect un-God God; to postulate such a thing makes nonsense out of everything. At the same time, this passage is *not a hypothetical warning* for the members of the church. This is a real letter, written in real time, to a group of baptized Christians who were contemplating real apostasy. So how are we to reconcile these two elements? God's decrees are sure, and these Christians here might fall away.

In order to consider the nature of apostasy, we have to consider the nature of the church. What is the "real" church? Since the Reformation, Protestants have been accustomed to speak of the *invisible* church and the *visible* church. The distinction is much older than the Reformation and actually goes back to Augustine. However, Augustine made a *series* of distinctions, not just one. For example, he also distinguished between the pilgrim church and the eschatological church. A series of layered distinctions helps us to understand the church from different angles instead of lapsing into an upper story/lower story dualism.

So while the distinction between the visible and invisible church communicates an important truth (one which we should heartily affirm), it can lead to misunderstandings and problems if it is affirmed as the *only* category for understanding the church. For example, given these "two" churches, which is the real one? Because evangelicals have answered (naturally) that the invisible church is the real one, this has led to the assumption that the visible church is, in some sense, unreal. This has led, in turn, to a disparagement of the visible church. Since the roster of names for the invisible church (the elect) differs from the roster of names for the visible church (all the church directories in the history of the world), then we would obviously give preference to the list that names the elect, in distinction from the list that includes Bishop Spong, lesbian pastors, and the BTK killer.

If I were to postulate a visible Suzy and an invisible Suzy, it makes sense to ask which one is the "real" one. If the church is the bride of Christ, *which* church is the bride of Christ? Evangelical Christians tend to say that the upper-story church is the bride of Christ, and this leads (whether we want it to or not) to the notion that the churches we attend on Sunday are nothing more than an earthly *approximation* of the church. But if we say, as we must, that the visible church and the invisible church are the same church, then this leads us to ask for a model that allows us to say this. Which is why I would return to another distinction of Augustine's—the pilgrim church and the eschatological church. The terms for this in recent discussion have been the historical church and the eschatological church.

If I speak about Suzy on Monday and Suzy on Friday, no one asks who the real Suzy is. It is the same Suzy at different points in time. This remains the case if we talk about Suzy on Monday, and Suzy at the Last Trump. The eschatological church *is the same church* as the historical church, and we have no problem accounting for why the roster of names is different. The eschatological church is the one true church with every blemish removed, and the historical church is the one true church without those blemishes removed yet.

So when someone is guilty of apostasy, he is falling away from the true church of Christ, of which he was genuinely a member. He was a genuine member, but not a permanent member. The permanent members of Christ's church are the elect. The blemishes that are removed from the bride of Christ were once part of her, but are no longer part of her. God, who knows the end from the beginning, knows who the elect are. He knows who will be part of the bride at the last day, and he decreed this before the first day. In the meantime, nothing is plainer in the New Testament than that non-elect people can be covenant members, and attached to Christ. In John 15, Jesus makes it very plain that branches can be *cut out of him*, taken away, and burned.

Always remember that apostasy is a real sin committed by real people who fall away from a real, visible church. The church they fall away from *is* the body of Christ, not an earthly attempt to approximate the body of Christ. The churches we worship in on the Lord's Day *are* the body of Christ.

Without understanding the reality of the covenant which makes up the covenant community of the church, we cannot possibly make sense of those passages in the New Testament which warn us about falling away. Either we hold to the eternal security and perseverance passages, and twist the covenant warning passages (as many Calvinists do), or we hold to the covenant warning passages, and twist the eternal security passages (as the Arminians do). *But all the Bible belongs to all Christians.* If we come to understand the doctrines of God's sovereignty over salvation, and the reality of Christ's covenant with the church, we can take all the Scriptures on these subjects *at face value.*

This means that the New Covenant is not a covenant without sanctions, without teeth. This means that the New Covenant contains with its ranks a class of people who are covenant-breakers. Those members of the covenant who are not elect (i.e., non-elect church members) receive genuine blessings which prepare them for stricter judgment. An unbelieving rejection of covenant blessings (held in possession) is the worst possible curse. These people have tasted the heavenly gift and the Word of God. As land they received the blessing of rain, but then decided to grow thorns with it. What will happen to them? They will come to *burning*. The law of Moses saw no curses as terrible as those curses which come upon apostate Christians. The modern baptistic mentality which tries to identify the New Covenant as the elect only does not know what to do with these warning passages, except turn them upside down.

According to the Bible, which is stricter—the word that came from Sinai or the word that comes from the heavenly Zion? Which causes greater trembling? Which should strike more awe in the believer's heart?

There remains a word of comfort. The author of Hebrews believes that this apostasy has not happened among his readers. He is convinced of "better things" in their case. However, this does not mean he believes the worse things to be impossible. (If he believed that, he would not needed to have written.) Nevertheless, he is encouraged about their prospects even though he speaks in this manner. And so should we, holding to the same faith, be encouraged.

STRONG CONSOLATION

If believers come away in despair from a study of the sixth chapter of Hebrews, this is an indication of a serious misreading of the text. This portion of Scripture provides some of the strongest comfort that can be found in the entire Bible.

> For God is not unjust so as to overlook your work and the love that you have shown for his name in serving the saints, as you still do. And we desire each one of you to show the same ear-

> nestness to have the full assurance of hope until the end, so that you may not be sluggish, but imitators of those who through faith and patience inherit the promises.
>
> For when God made a promise to Abraham, since he had no one greater by whom to swear, he swore by himself, saying, "Surely I will bless you and multiply you." And thus Abraham, having patiently waited, obtained the promise. For people swear by something greater than themselves, and in all their disputes an oath is final for confirmation. So when God desired to show more convincingly to the heirs of the promise the unchangeable character of his purpose, he guaranteed it with an oath, so that by two unchangeable things, in which it is impossible for God to lie, we who have fled for refuge might have strong encouragement to hold fast to the hope set before us. We have this as a sure and steadfast anchor of the soul, a hope that enters into the inner place behind the curtain, where Jesus has gone as a forerunner on our behalf, having become a high priest forever after the order of Melchizedek. (Heb. 6:10–20)

The warnings in the first part of the chapter are warnings against true covenant apostasy, but they are not consistent with those things which "accompany salvation" (v. 9). What, then, *does* accompany salvation? *Full assurance* of hope until the end (v. 11), faithful and patient inheritance of the *promises* (v. 12), the *unchangeable nature* of God's intent to save (v. 17), *strong encouragement* for heirs of this hope (v. 18), and an *anchor of the soul*, sure and steadfast (v. 19).

So the sixth chapter of Hebrews is the great chapter on the everlasting security of the one who through faith trusts in Christ. Is every covenant member such an heir? No—that is why the covenant warnings are present in the first part of the chapter. But those covenant members with true faith in Christ are not left to twist in the wind.

We must remember the context of this book. Three things are worth remembering about the language of Hebrews. Remember the destruction of Jerusalem, which will occur within a very short period of time after the writing of this letter. These are people contemplating a return to a religion centered in Jerusalem, which was about to be destroyed in the raging fire that would consume the adversaries of God. Remember the corporate *plural* language in the early warnings—the land drinking in the rain is the vineyard of the Lord, which is the church and not the individual heart. And third, recall that the issue is *visible apostasy*, not invisible "sins against the Holy Ghost."

The strength of our consolation here is based entirely upon God's character. God does not change. We have been given two immutable things—God's character does not change, and consequently his Word does not change. In order that we could have an even stronger hope, God swore by himself—his oath cannot change either. So now we have fled to this refuge, the refuge of God's immutability in his purpose of saving us (v. 18).

Think for a moment. If our salvation were what most Christians assume it to be—a cooperative effort between God and man—how does this provide *strong encouragement*? This reduces the whole sorry affair to "you will never be lost if *you* . . ." If God has immutably decreed that we will not be lost if *we* . . . , then where are we? Not only are we without strong consolation, we are without any consolation at all. A chain, including the chain of salvation, is only as strong as its weakest link. Are you one of those links? Or do you glory in the fact that you are not?

Look *away*. Away from your heart, away from your sins, away from your doubts, away from your trials, away from your motives, away from *yourself*. Outside Jerusalem, two thousand years ago, Christ was hung on the cross *to accomplish God's immutable purposes in salvation*. "Yes, but I want to know if I am a part of that salvation. Does it include me?" If you really want to know, then look *away*. Look to *Christ*. Those who do, see him. Those who do not are left with their own goodness and only enough attachment to the covenant to make them miserable.

10

Abraham and Melchizedek

We must prepare our minds to think as mature Christians. The author of Hebrews wanted very much for us to be able to follow his argument here. Without spiritual maturity, grounded in practical obedience, we will not be able to get what he is driving at. When Jesus gave the Great Commission, the thing he said to do was to disciple the nations, baptizing them, and teaching them obedience. He did not say to teach them to spew facts; he said that our task is the inculcation of *obedience*.

> For this Melchizedek, king of Salem, priest of the Most High God, met Abraham returning from the slaughter of the kings and blessed him, and to him Abraham apportioned a tenth part of everything. He is first, by translation of his name, king of right-

> eousness, and then he is also king of Salem, that is, king of peace. He is without father or mother or genealogy, having neither beginning of days nor end of life, but resembling the Son of God he continues a priest forever.
>
> See how great this man was to whom Abraham the patriarch gave a tenth of the spoils! And those descendants of Levi who receive the priestly office have a commandment in the law to take tithes from the people, that is, from their brothers, though these also are descended from Abraham. But this man who does not have his descent from them received tithes from Abraham and blessed him who had the promises. It is beyond dispute that the inferior is blessed by the superior. In the one case tithes are received by mortal men, but in the other case, by one of whom it is testified that he lives. One might even say that Levi himself, who receives tithes, paid tithes through Abraham, for he was still in the loins of his ancestor when Melchizedek met him. (Heb. 7:1–10)

We are introduced to an ancient king. In olden time, Melchizedek was a king of Salem (an early name for Jerusalem). He was also a priest of the Most High God. The Hebrew word *melek* means *king*, and *zedek* means *righteousness*. This enigmatic figure is named in Genesis, and then again in the psalms. The author of Hebrews shows us that the structure of the sacred text itself is a prophetic type. Without father or mother *in the text*, without birth or death *in the text*, without genealogy *in the text*, he provides a great picture of the Son of God. We know that he was not a theophany, an Old Testament appearance of Christ, because he is compared *to* Christ ("*resembling* the Son of God," v. 3), and because Jesus Christ *became* a Melchizedekan priest (6:20).

We learn something here about authority and submission. The argument here is that Melchizedek is much greater than Abraham—even though Abraham had the promises. This is seen in the fact that Melchizedek blessed Abraham (and the greater always blesses the lesser), and in the fact that Abraham tithed to Melchizedek. Not only was this so, but Abraham's descendants, still in his loins by federal representation, were represented in that tithe. This means the Levitical priesthood is *less than* the Melchizedekan priesthood. And remember the point of this letter. The point is the greatness of Christ's person and office, indeed the supremacy of his person and office.

Notice that Melchizedek delivered his blessing immediately after Abraham, a great man of war, slaughtered some very grievous enemies of righteousness. Abraham pursued Chedorlaomer and destroyed him because he had taken Lot captive. Abraham was met by Melchizedek and the king of Sodom. Abraham gave a tenth of the spoil to Melchizedek and refused to keep the remainder—*that* he returned to the king of Sodom. Abraham was a military man, and he honored the Lord with the spoils of his victory.

This exchange predates the *incorporation* of the tithe into the Mosaic code. In this respect it is like the Sabbath, or circumcision. These things were not part of the Mosaic code only. This indicates that the tithe is grounded in the way things are and is not just an administrative detail. We still observe the sabbath in the Lord's Day (Heb. 4:10), and we still observe circumcision through baptism (Col. 2:11). The difference is that the tithe is still honored in the same manner that it was before—ten percent is still ten percent.

We do not mind it when God demonstrates his greatness by blessing us. We do mind (sinfully) having to declare his greatness ourselves through the tithe. But the two *go together*. Nothing in the New Testament indicates that the practice of tithing is set aside, any more than our inferiority and Christ's greatness is set aside. If the relation still stands, why not this biblical way of declaring the relation? We do not give ten percent as a way of showing that ninety percent remains "ours." Rather, just as we observe the Lord's Day, so we render the tithe. We set one day out of seven apart, not because the remaining six belong to us, but rather as a way of rendering the firstfruits. We are declaring, by offering one, that the other six are his as well. We offer ten percent as a ritual signification that one hundred percent is the Lord's. We do not pay the money because we have extra and God is always a little short. We offer him tribute. The earth is the Lord's and the fullness thereof. All we have and are belong to him. We tend to forget this, to our dismay and sorrow, and so God has instituted this little reminder. Ten percent, and off the top.

The Bible teaches that the "Levitical office" continues in some form under the New Covenant. "And some of them also I will take for priests and for Levites, says the LORD" (Is. 66:21). In the New Covenant, priests and Levites (ministers) are taken from among the Gentiles. One of the features that carries over to support the work of Levitical Gentiles is this one: "Do you not know that those who are employed in the temple service get their food from the temple, and those who serve at the altar share in the sacrificial offerings? *In the same way*, the Lord commanded that those who proclaim the gospel should get their living by the gospel" (1 Cor. 9:13–14). The "in the same way" here means that ministers are paid "the same way." Those who minister under the New Covenant are to receive their living *in the same way* as the Levites did in the Old. What was that "way"? It was the tithe.

All the financial embarrassments which afflict the church of Christ can be traced back to this. We do not declare the supremacy of Christ in this fundamental way. We will lay *anything* at his feet conceptually—except for our hidden idol. Tithing is one of the few ways to really mortify the idol of consumerism and materialism that genuinely afflicts Christians in the West today. Talk about the Lordship of Jesus, the supremacy of Jesus, without honoring him with the firstfruits of your labor, is just that: talk. Abraham demonstrated the supremacy of Melchizedek, and he did not do this by asking Melchizedek into his heart. He did not do it by developing a "personal relationship" with Melchizedek.

NO SACRIFICE REMAINS

The author of Hebrews continues his comparison between the priestly order of Melchizedek and the priestly order of Levi. As we shall see, understanding the difference makes an immense practical difference.

> Now if perfection had been attainable through the Levitical priesthood (for under it the people received the law), what further need would there have been for another priest to arise after the order of Melchizedek, rather than one named after the order of Aaron? For when there is a change in the priesthood, there is necessarily a change in the law as well. For the one of whom

these things are spoken belonged to another tribe, from which no one has ever served at the altar. For it is evident that our Lord was descended from Judah, and in connection with that tribe Moses said nothing about priests.

This becomes even more evident when another priest arises in the likeness of Melchizedek, who has become a priest, not on the basis of a legal requirement concerning bodily descent, but by the power of an indestructible life. For it is witnessed of him,

> "You are a priest forever,
> after the order of Melchizedek."

For on the one hand, a former commandment is set aside because of its weakness and uselessness (for the law made nothing perfect); but on the other hand, a better hope is introduced, through which we draw near to God.

And it was not without an oath. For those who formerly became priests were made such without an oath, but this one was made a priest with an oath by the one who said to him:

> "The Lord has sworn
> and will not change his mind,
> 'You are a priest forever.' "

This makes Jesus the guarantor of a better covenant.

The former priests were many in number, because they were prevented by death from continuing in office, but he holds his priesthood permanently, because he continues forever. Consequently, he is able to save to the uttermost those who draw near to God through him, since he always lives to make intercession for them.

For it was indeed fitting that we should have such a high priest, holy, innocent, unstained, separated from sinners, and exalted above the heavens. He has no need, like those high priests, to offer sacrifices daily, first for his own sins and then for those of the people, since he did this once for all when he offered up himself. For the law appoints men in their weakness as high priests, but

> the word of the oath, which came later than the law, appoints a Son who has been made perfect forever. (Heb. 7:11–28)

In the first section of this passage (vv. 11–19), we see the inadequacy of the Levitical priesthood. In verses 20 through 24, we see the two priesthoods contrasted, with Christ's marked as immeasurably superior. In the last section (vv. 25–28) the application of the doctrine is made.

We are dealing with a change in the law. The recipients of this letter were considering "going back." But if perfection, or completeness, were to be found there, back where they were going, then why did David prophesy *another* kind of priest? It is not possible, the author of Hebrews argues, to have a change in the priesthood without having a corresponding change in the law which governs that priesthood (v. 13). The word used for *change* here means to "put one thing in place of another," or, as we would say, "change out." This means that the older Levitical system knew and understood itself to be temporary and provisional. The Old Testament prophesies the necessity of the New. If a man who knew nothing of the Christian faith, Judaism, or the history of the church were given a copy of the Old Testament, and he read it carefully, his first question would be, "Where's part two?"

Nevertheless, this change from the old Levitical system was very difficult to the Jews who had "done it this way" for many centuries. They got attached to the provisional system as though it were the permanent set-up. In desperation, some Jewish Christians might be tempted to do some genealogical research on behalf of the Lord—"maybe we can get him (somehow) into the tribe of Levi." But our writer heads off any and all such attempts. Our Lord was from the tribe of Judah.

In the following section, we find more evidence that Christ is not identical with Melchizedek. He arises as "another priest" in the *likeness* of Melchizedek. In contrast to the sons of Aaron, his power does not come from law that governs what we do here and now, but rather his authority comes from an endless life. "You are a priest *forever*" (v. 17). Consequently he annuls a weak and unprofitable commandment—that which consisted of the system of one

Levitical priest replacing another.

This brings us to the everlasting oath. The two priesthoods are then compared and contrasted, with the priesthood according to Melchizedek shown to be immeasurably higher. The author of Hebrews has already shown that the father of the Levites paid tithes to Melchizedek. Here he goes further. The Lord was made a priest *by an oath* (vv. 20–21), unlike the Levitical priests; "The Lord has *sworn*. . ." The Lord, having risen everlastingly from the dead, never needs to be replaced, unlike the Levitical priests (vv. 23–24).

The result is that we may conclude that the Lord is the *guarantor* of a better covenant (v. 22). The word "guarantor" gives a sense of what is about to be said concerning our salvation. The word means that the Lord is the *sponsor*, the true *guarantee* of our salvation.

This is the basis of "salvation to the uttermost." Jesus Christ is able to save *completely*. "Consequently, he is able to save to the uttermost those who draw near to God through him, since he always lives to make intercession for them" (v. 25). The word for *uttermost* is a great adverb in the Greek and means "utterly, completely, perfectly." When Christ saves, there is nothing left to be done; all that remains is the simple application of what he has done by the Holy Spirit.

In this text, we identify those whom he saves in this way (those who come to God through him), and we identify them on the basis of that salvation—*his* ability to make intercession. And his intercession as Priest is based upon his sacrifice as Lamb. The greatness of our salvation must never be detached from the greatness of our Savior. "For it was indeed fitting that we should have such a high priest, holy, innocent, unstained, separated from sinners, and exalted above the heavens" (v. 26). The writer of Hebrews says something profound in the next verse. Christ does not need to offer up sacrifices daily. And why not? He doesn't need to offer daily sacrifices for his own sins because he doesn't have any. He doesn't need to offer daily sacrifices for us "since *he did this* once for all when he offered up himself" (v. 27). Our salvation is based upon the glorious premise that *no sacrifice for sins remains*. This is one of our central blessings.

11

Christ the Liturgist

We have already discussed the importance of defining the word *covenant* correctly. We must also define the adjective *new* in the phrase "New Covenant" correctly. A host of errors have sprung from the fact that we have misdefined this simple word *new*. We are under the "New Covenant." What does that mean exactly?

In the eighth chapter of Hebrews we are taught that Christ is our high priest. He serves in the heavenly tabernacle, and not at all in the earthly tabernacle. The prophet Jeremiah predicted that God would bring this to pass, and would make a new covenant with the houses of Israel and Judah. The fault with the older covenant was with the people, not with the covenant, but the heavenly covenant is founded on better promises—promises which take our sinfulness into account, promises which *conquer* our sinfulness. In this New Covenant we find the internalization of the law. The Old Covenant is on its last legs, and is about ready to vanish away.

> Now the point in what we are saying is this: we have such a high priest, one who is seated at the right hand of the throne of the Majesty in heaven, a minister in the holy places, in the true tent that the Lord set up, not man. For every high priest is appointed to offer gifts and sacrifices; thus it is necessary for this priest also to have something to offer. Now if he were on earth, he would not be a priest at all, since there are priests who offer gifts according to the law. They serve a copy and shadow of the heavenly things. For when Moses was about to erect the tent, he was instructed by God, saying, "See that you make everything according to the pattern that was shown you on the mountain." But as it is, Christ has obtained a ministry that is as much more excellent than the old as the covenant he mediates is better, since it is enacted on better promises. For if that first covenant had been faultless, there would have been no occasion to look for a second.
>
> For he finds fault with them when he says:
>
> "Behold, the days are coming, declares the Lord,
> when I will establish a new covenant with the house of Israel
> and with the house of Judah,
> not like the covenant that I made with their fathers
> on the day when I took them by the hand to bring them out of the land of Egypt.
> For they did not continue in my covenant,
> and so I showed no concern for them, declares the Lord.
> For this is the covenant that I will make with the house of Israel
> after those days, declares the Lord:
> I will put my laws into their minds,
> and write them on their hearts,
> and I will be their God,
> and they shall be my people.
> And they shall not teach, each one his neighbor
> and each one his brother, saying, 'Know the Lord,'

> for they shall all know me,
> from the least of them to the greatest.
> For I will be merciful toward their iniquities,
> and I will remember their sins no more."
>
> In speaking of a new covenant, he makes the first one obsolete. And what is becoming obsolete and growing old is ready to vanish away. (Heb. 8:1–13)

Sometimes the scriptural writers help us understand how to structure the points of the book they have given us. They say things like, "Now this is the main point of the things we are saying . . ." (v. 1). And so what is that main point? We have a forever priest, with his work completed, *seated* at the right hand of God's Majesty. He is the minister of the sanctuary and the true tabernacle. The word for minister is the one from which we get *liturgy*. Our Lord is the great liturgist of heaven. More than this, our Lord is the ultimate liturgy himself.

From the definition of priest we know that he must have something to offer, but from the fact of how the law regulates offerings, if he were an earthly priest, he would have nothing to offer. He was from the tribe of Judah, not Levi. The earthly priests offer up shadow sacrifices in a shadow tabernacle. Christ offered up a true sacrifice in the heavenly tabernacle.

This is where we begin to see the importance of the word *new*. We must not understand our New Covenant in an earthly way. The Old Covenant was copied from something *already existent* in the heavens—the true tabernacle in which Christ now serves. *Old* and *New* are not coupled together in time like two railroad cars. The *New* and the "second" ministry was the one Moses was instructed *to copy*. ". . . [t]hey serve a copy and shadow of the heavenly things . . ." (v. 5). When we say New Covenant we should understand this as *heavenly covenant*. When we say Old Covenant we should understand *heavenly shadow covenant*.

The New Covenant was operative throughout the period of the Old Covenant. *The Old Covenant was a copy of it*. Those who understand the New Covenant as something beginning at a certain point in time a mere two thousand years ago do not understand that the covenant is different *in kind*, and not merely different in time sequence. This covenant, like the priest who is the minister of this covenant, is "without beginning of days or end of life." The New Covenant does not start in time—although it does come to fruition and fulfillment in time.

These are better promises. Christ has obtained a more excellent service, or liturgy. It is the liturgy of *sitting down*. His sacrifice and his offering have been completed, and he is seated at the right hand of the Majesty in heaven. If the ministry of constant repetition had been adequate, then no need for Jeremiah's prophecy would exist. But Jeremiah says plainly that a new covenant will have to be made. This New Covenant has better promises—promises which actually deal with us.

With whom is the covenant made? The covenant is made with the house of Israel and the house of Judah. This is very important. Unless you belong to these two houses, the covenant is not for you. You are a true Jew if your heart is circumcised, a citizen in the *heavenly* Jerusalem. Every Christian must therefore be a heavenly Israelite.

Another feature of this covenant is the matter of heart law. The terms of the covenant are two-fold. The first feature is the internalization of the law—which is not the same thing as the vaporization of the law. The second feature is forgiveness of sins. With regard to the first, we know that sin is lawlessness. We know that Christ has taken the requirement of the law and written them on the tablets of human hearts (2 Cor. 3:1–6).

With regard to the second, Christianity is a faith that is open only to screw-ups. Without forgiveness of sins, we would all be helpless and hopeless. Those who are content with how they currently are have no knowledge of genuine faith.

12

Blood and Judgment

The outer sanctuary is the place where preparations are made for the entry to the inner Holy of Holies. And so we learn about Christ's ministry in the heavenly Holy of Holies through the activity in the outer sanctuary, that is, the time of the Old Testament.

> For where a will is involved, the death of the one who made it must be established. For a will takes effect only at death, since it is not in force as long as the one who made it is alive. Therefore not even the first covenant was inaugurated without blood. For when every commandment of the law had been declared by Moses to all the people, he took the blood of calves and goats, with water and scarlet wool and hyssop, and sprinkled both the book itself and all the people, saying, "This is the blood of the

> covenant that God commanded for you." And in the same way he sprinkled with the blood both the tent and all the vessels used in worship. Indeed, under the law almost everything is purified with blood, and without the shedding of blood there is no forgiveness of sins.
>
> Thus it was necessary for the copies of the heavenly things to be purified with these rites, but the heavenly things themselves with better sacrifices than these. For Christ has entered, not into holy places made with hands, which are copies of the true things, but into heaven itself, now to appear in the presence of God on our behalf. Nor was it to offer himself repeatedly, as the high priest enters the holy places every year with blood not his own, for then he would have had to suffer repeatedly since the foundation of the world. But as it is, he has appeared once for all at the end of the ages to put away sin by the sacrifice of himself. And just as it is appointed for man to die once, and after that comes judgment, so Christ, having been offered once to bear the sins of many, will appear a second time, not to deal with sin but to save those who are eagerly waiting for him. (Heb. 9:16–28)

Given the nature of "testaments," a death is necessary in order for the will and testament to take effect. The author of Hebrews shows us here that a comparison exists between a *testament* and a *covenant*. In just the way that a death is necessary for a testament, so also death was necessary for the ratification or dedication of the first covenant. Remember that a covenant is a solemn bond, sovereignly administered, with attendant blessings and curses. When the covenant is between God and man, it is a solemn bond, sovereignly administered, *sealed in blood*, with attendant blessings and curses.

This brings us back to the sprinkling of blood. In the earlier part of this chapter, the author spoke of *baptisms*. Here he gives some examples of these baptisms. Moses sprinkled blood on both the people and the book of the covenant, as well as the articles used in the ministry of worship. Everything was purified with blood. According to the law, without the shedding of blood, there is no remission of sin. We must therefore emphasize that *the Christian faith is a religion founded on blood sacrifice*. Moreover the shedding of blood in the older covenant was not intended to be efficacious, but rather typological through animals. The Christian faith is built on the foundation of a human sacrifice but in the Old Covenant it was animals. If sin is to be dealt with, blood must flow. To the modernist, this seems barbaric—but it deals with the fact of sin. The only way to avoid blood sacrifice in religion is to traffic in wishful thinking.

Scripture teaches us here that the tabernacle in the heavens needed to be purified. Because it is in the heavens, only the blood of Christ would suffice to accomplish this. The blood of bulls and goats could purify the tabernacle here, but in the heavenlies only the true and ultimate sacrifice was worthy.

This relates to our sense of Christian finality. Christ came at the "end of the ages." An air of finality attended his arrival, his ministry, his work. His work was *to put away sin*. Christ was offered *one time* in the same way that each man dies *one time*. First is the death, an event in history, and after the death follow the consequences of the nature of that death. Christ died for the many, and after that death, their sins were put away. Each man dies in history, and after that follows the judgment. Nothing is more certain than the inevitability of your death, and nothing is more certain than the judgment that will follow that death. The question each one of us must ask ourselves regularly is this: Do we have a high priest who has put away our sins? Do we have a sacrifice in the heavens? Do we have *Christ*?

13

Covenant Boldness and Covenant Fear

The tenth chapter of Hebrews really needs to be considered all together. In this chapter we find a great deal of the theology of our author coming together as part of an integrated whole. If we step back and get the big picture, we will see more than just the tenth chapter—we will begin to see the entire book.

That is part of the reason for commenting on such large portions of Hebrews in this commentary. If we look at everything under a microscope, we frequently miss the elephant. In this chapter we have one of the best examples found in Scripture where the meaning of the text *cannot* be ascertained apart from the immediate historical context. Not only is this the case, but when that context is explained and set out, many blurry things in the book of Hebrews suddenly come into sharp focus. It is like watching an impressionist painting turn into a painting from the photo-realism school. In order to get at this, it is best to read through the entire chapter at one go.

For since the law has but a shadow of the good things to come instead of the true form of these realities, it can never, by the same sacrifices that are continually offered every year, make perfect those who draw near. Otherwise, would they not have ceased to be offered, since the worshipers, having once been cleansed, would no longer have any consciousness of sins? But in these sacrifices there is a reminder of sins every year. For it is impossible for the blood of bulls and goats to take away sins.

Consequently, when Christ came into the world, he said,

> "Sacrifices and offerings you have not desired,
>   but a body have you prepared for me;
> in burnt offerings and sin offerings
>   you have taken no pleasure.
> Then I said, 'Behold, I have come to do your will, O God,
>   as it is written of me in the scroll of the book.' "

When he said above, "You have neither desired nor taken pleasure in sacrifices and offerings and burnt offerings and sin offerings" (these are offered according to the law), then he added, "Behold, I have come to do your will." He does away with the first in order to establish the second. And by that will we have been sanctified through the offering of the body of Jesus Christ once for all.

And every priest stands daily at his service, offering repeatedly the same sacrifices, which can never take away sins. But when Christ had offered for all time a single sacrifice for sins, he sat down at the right hand of God, waiting from that time until his enemies should be made a footstool for his feet. For by a single offering he has perfected for all time those who are being sanctified.

And the Holy Spirit also bears witness to us; for after saying,

> "This is the covenant that I will make with them
>   after those days, declares the Lord:
> I will put my laws on their hearts,
>   and write them on their minds,"

then he adds,

"I will remember their sins and their lawless deeds no more."

Where there is forgiveness of these, there is no longer any offering for sin.

Therefore, brothers, since we have confidence to enter the holy places by the blood of Jesus, by the new and living way that he opened for us through the curtain, that is, through his flesh, and since we have a great priest over the house of God, let us draw near with a true heart in full assurance of faith, with our hearts sprinkled clean from an evil conscience and our bodies washed with pure water. Let us hold fast the confession of our hope without wavering, for he who promised is faithful. And let us consider how to stir up one another to love and good works, not neglecting to meet together, as is the habit of some, but encouraging one another, and all the more as you see the Day drawing near.

For if we go on sinning deliberately after receiving the knowledge of the truth, there no longer remains a sacrifice for sins, but a fearful expectation of judgment, and a fury of fire that will consume the adversaries. Anyone who has set aside the law of Moses dies without mercy on the evidence of two or three witnesses. How much worse punishment, do you think, will be deserved by the one who has spurned the Son of God, and has profaned the blood of the covenant by which he was sanctified, and has outraged the Spirit of grace? For we know him who said, "Vengeance is mine; I will repay." And again, "The Lord will judge his people." It is a fearful thing to fall into the hands of the living God.

But recall the former days when, after you were enlightened, you endured a hard struggle with sufferings, sometimes being publicly exposed to reproach and affliction, and sometimes being partners with those so treated. For you had compassion on those in prison, and you joyfully accepted the plundering of your property, since you knew that you yourselves had a better possession and an abiding one. Therefore do not throw away your confidence, which has a great reward. For you have need of endurance, so that when you have done the will of God you may receive what is promised.

For,

> "Yet a little while,
>   and the coming one will come and will not delay;
> but my righteous one shall live by faith,
>   and if he shrinks back,
> my soul has no pleasure in him."

But we are not of those who shrink back and are destroyed, but of those who have faith and preserve their souls. (Heb. 10:1–39)

Now shadows of the reality cannot do what the reality can. The true sacrifice cannot be offered in the outer sanctuary—that is reserved for the inner Most Holy Place. In the first four verses of this chapter we have a reiteration of what we have been learning in the ninth chapter—the necessary repetition of the Levitical sacrifices reveals the central problem with them. These sacrifices were a successful shadow (vv. 1–4). The shadows repeat themselves, and as they do so, they are being good shadows, but they are also revealing that they are not themselves the reality.

Even though these blood sacrifices were offered according to the law (and therefore were according to God's will), God still told the people in Psalm 40:6–8 that he had no pleasure in the sacrifices. He followed this with Christ saying that he had come to do God's will, to do God's pleasure. This indicates the priority that Christ's sacrifice has over that of bulls and goats. God takes away the animal sacrifices to replace them with the once-for-all sacrifice of Christ (vv. 5–9).

Those who have been blessed with the grace of God described here have been made perfect forever. When God fulfilled his pleasure, the result was a perfect "setting apart" of his people. Consider: "And by that will we have been sanctified through the offering of the body of Jesus Christ once for all" (v. 10). "For by a single offering he has perfected for all time those who are being sanctified" (v. 14). We have a perfect sanctification here—a definitive sanctification.

Christ has been seated at God's right hand. This seating indicates four things: He is waiting for his enemies to be made his footstool (vv. 12–13); he has sanctified a certain class of people forever

(vv. 10, 14); he has established the New Covenant (vv. 16–17); and he has annihilated sin offerings (v. 18). This last is crucial for understanding verse 26.

The end result is a sprinkled heart. The outcome of this theology is confidence before the throne of God. The blood of Jesus has opened the veil to the Holy of Holies, which is the flesh of Jesus. Now we have a high priest forever, and we are exhorted to draw near with full assurance. Our hearts have been sprinkled with the blood, and our bodies have been washed in baptism. So we are to hold fast, not so that we can be faithful, but rather because *he* is faithful. This and only this is the basis of love, good works, and church attendance (vv. 24–25).

Now this is the place where context matters so much, and where, if we grasp that context, the lights come on. Remember that the elect have been made perfect forever. However, we still must deal with those who are covenantally attached to Christ, but who do not know him in truth. The "sinning deliberately" cannot be understood apart from the context of the first century, at which time some Christian Jews were attempting to go back to the blood of bulls and goats (v. 26). They are warned (again) that Jerusalem is going to burn—no sense going back there (v. 27). Contrast two differently contextualized paraphrases of verse 26.

Time—anywhere in Christian history: "For if we sin deliberately by reading *Penthouse* after we have received the knowledge of the truth that to do so is a violation of the seventh commandment *and* the Sermon on the Mount, there no longer remains a sacrifice for our lustful sins, meaning that Jesus didn't die for heart-adulterers like us, but all that awaits us is a certain fearful expectation of the final judgment, and the fiery indignation of hell which will devour the adversaries" (v. 26).

Time—about 66 AD, just before the war broke out that destroyed Jerusalem, prophesied by Jesus to happen within one generation of 30 AD. In other words, when Hebrews was written, about ten minutes to midnight: "For if we sin deliberately by returning to the Levitical sacrifices, which must be offered in Jerusalem (which means in turn that we have to get on the boat and go there, just in time for the war), after we have received the knowledge of the truth that Christ died once for all, putting an end to these repetitive sacrifices in doomed Jerusalem, there no longer remains a sacrifice for sins back in Jerusalem where we are thinking to go, but a certain fearful expectation of judgment, catapults, Roman armies, forests of crucified Jews, and fiery indignation which will devour the adversaries, just as Jesus prophesied" (v. 26).

An illustration I have used before is this: suppose the gift of prophecy were still operative today, and a prophet stood up in our church and predicted that within two years Salt Lake City was going to be destroyed by a giant meteor crashing into the earth. We know that our prophet is a good guy named Agabus, and so we know this is going to happen. Then, in a masterpiece of bad timing, a college student in our church with a Mormon background announces that his family has told him that if he forgets all this evangelical, born-again business, they will set him up in business (in Salt Lake City), get him a cute LDS wife, and really take care of him. For various reasons, let us say that our young man is wavering, and he is really considering it.

Now of course, we are concerned about his soul. But our pleading with him is going to be greatly affected by our knowledge that he is contemplating moving to a city that is going to be squashed by a giant rock from space within a matter of months. We are not just concerned about judgment at the end of the world (though that is an important part of all this), but we are *also* concerned about temporal, historical judgment, about to happen, here and now. This is exactly the kind of situation that the author of Hebrews was facing. Some Jewish Christians suddenly started to waver in their faith, and were thinking of going back to Jerusalem to worship, when that city was on the very threshold of her destruction. The whole Christian church knew of that pending destruction—Jesus could not have been plainer. The mid-to-late sixties was a bad time to take up the practice of sacrificing bulls and goats in the temple at Jerusalem.

We see in all this that the New Covenant contains fearful curses indeed—far worse than the curses of the Old Covenant. It is a fearful thing for a covenant member to fall into the hands of the living God (vv. 29–31). We are warned of a *far worse* punishment than the Jews of the older covenant faced. So we are to live up to what we have already attained. Notice the exhortation here. The author of Hebrews tells them to recall "the former days." They are not told to pry into the Book of Life to try to find out if they are elect. Our election is confirmed by our knowledge here, in this life, of how we live (vv. 32–39).

FORGIVEN AND FORGIVING

The Lord Jesus was born into a *sinful* world. His advent was not designed as an inspirational moment to crown all the others, but rather he was sent as a *Savior*. He came to bring forgiveness, and consequently if there is anything his followers should understand and practice, it is forgiveness. " 'This is the covenant that I will make with them after those days, declares the Lord: I will put my laws on their hearts, and write them on their minds.' Then he adds, 'I will remember their sins and their lawless deeds no more.' Where there is forgiveness of these, there is no longer any offering for sin" (Heb. 10:16–18).

"And her husband Joseph, being a just man and unwilling to put her to shame, resolved to divorce her quietly. But as he considered these things, behold, an angel of the Lord appeared to him in a dream, saying, 'Joseph, son of David, do not fear to take Mary as your wife, for that which is conceived in her is from the Holy Spirit. She will bear a son, and you shall call his name Jesus, for he will save his people from their sins' " (Matt. 1:19–21).

After Joseph discovered that Mary was pregnant (and he knew that *he* wasn't the father), the only reasonable conclusion to draw was that Mary had been unfaithful (Matt. 1:19). He did not want to humiliate her, so he resolved to divorce her quietly. While he was deciding what to do, an angel appeared to him in a dream, called him a son of David, and told him that Mary had conceived as a result of the work of the Holy Spirit (v. 20). The angel told him, further, that the baby would be a boy and that Joseph was to name him Jesus. The reason for the name is that he would save his people from their sins (v. 21). The name *Jesus* is the New Testament equivalent of *Joshua*, "God is salvation," a meaning that Matthew confirms, adding the important detail that the salvation is from sin.

Jeremiah had looked forward to the coming of the New Covenant—a time when Israel and Judah would be transformed into covenant-keepers. In Hebrews 8, the entire passage from Jeremiah is quoted. In Hebrews 10, it is quoted again in abridged form, emphasizing the key details of the new covenants. These key terms were the internalization of the law (Heb. 10:16) and the forgiveness of sins (v. 16). And where there is remission, there is no further need for sin offerings (v. 17).

We are dealing here with deep forgiveness. The Lord Jesus did not come, live a perfect life, and die on the cross and come back from the dead in order to dab around the edges of our wound. Our complicity in the sin of Adam and our continuing screwed-up-ness required a great remedy which could not be had apart from the work of a great Savior. Remember that Jesus is saving us from our *sins*, and not merely from the *consequences* of our sins. One of the central sins he is saving us from is the sin of the double standard—wanting to receive forgiveness on easy terms, and wanting to extend it with the heart of a stickler for justice. We want to borrow easily, and lend with difficulty. We want our fingers open to receive, and our fist clenched for giving. Yet Jesus has given us fair warning that we do not receive forgiveness on our terms. Not at all. In the Lord's prayer, we are taught to say this to *God*—"And forgive us our debts, as we also have forgiven our debtors" (Matt. 6:12). "Dear God, please harbor toward me all the thoughts I harbor toward others." Do the words stick in the throat? "So also my heavenly Father will do to every one of you, if you do not forgive your brother from your heart" (Matt. 18:21–35). Forgiving others is *not optional*.

This is the very heart of the *gospel* message. "God exalted him at his right hand as Leader and Savior, to give repentance to Israel and *forgiveness of sins*" (Acts 5:31). "Let it be known to you therefore, brothers, that through this man *forgiveness of sins is proclaimed to you*" (Acts 13:38). ". . . to open their eyes, so that they may turn from darkness to light and from the power of Satan to God, *that they may receive forgiveness of sins* and a place among those who are sanctified by faith in me" (Acts 26:18). "In him we have redemption through his blood, *the forgiveness of our trespasses*, according to the riches of his grace" (Eph. 1:7; cf. Col. 1:14).

We usually have a better understanding of forgiveness when receiving it, because we *need* the forgiveness we receive to be all-encompassing. We want to receive forgiveness dispensed from a fire hose, and we want to ladle it out with a teaspoon. But Jesus came to save us from our parsimonious selves. Forgiveness means treating the other person as though they did absolutely no wrong—even though you know that they did. Forgiveness presupposes real sin. You don't have to kid yourself to be forgiving—in fact, it is crucial not to. "I'll forgive him because he didn't really mean it" is whitewash, not forgiveness.

Having been forgiven for everything, we must have hearts that are completely and entirely full of forgiveness for those who have wronged us. Still, the world is a messy place—what does this *look* like? First, love and forgiveness cover a multitude of sins (1 Pet. 4:8). This means that forgiveness (for a certain kind of sin) *can* be extended without the other person's cooperation, but this "cover" has to be a cleansing carpet, not a lumpy one. Second, love and forgiveness do not attempt to read the heart (Luke 17:3–5). We are told to forgive, up to seven times daily, which actually means four hundred ninety times, and this applies even though all of us would have our suspicions that the repentance wasn't genuine about the third or fourth time. Forgiveness is a *transaction*, like the sale of a mule. Third, love and forgiveness confront when necessary (Matt. 18:15–19). This must only be pursued for the sake of the other person, not your own sake. It is quite striking that Jesus tells the parable of the unmerciful servant immediately after the famous "Matthew 18" instruction. But both these teachings are in Matthew 18. The unmerciful servant is the one sinned against, and so he would have been the one following the Matthew 18 court process. Conservative believers are far more *comfortable* with accusation than they ought to be. Run a thought experiment concerning two hundred Christian law students who have just passed the bar. One hundred of them are going to be defense attorneys and one hundred will be prosecutors. Which group will be asked to justify their choice of a profession with their Christian faith?

14

Bible Stories

One fatal tendency is to assume that Bible stories are for children and that doctrine is for adults. But in fact the entire Bible is for all Christians. One of the lamentable results of biblical illiteracy is the fact that many Christians could not tell you what happened to all the saints mentioned in this chapter. However, as we learn our Bible stories, we learn the centrality of *faith*. There is no opposition between robust narrative and doctrinal faith.

> Now faith is the assurance of things hoped for, the conviction of things not seen. For by it the people of old received their commendation. . . . (Heb. 11:1–40)

We begin with the story of creation, which (not surprisingly) is where unbelievers also begin their competing story. "By faith we understand that the universe was created by the word of God, so that what is seen was not made out of things that are visible" (v. 3). Faith for anything in the Christian life begins with our faith in the living and *creator* God. All this evolution foolishness (and various Christian compromises with it) is nothing less than an assault on the entire Christian faith. You cannot assault the first story without attacking the entire building.

We then come to Abel and Enoch. Both these men had faith. Abel's righteous sacrifice was received and Cain's was not, and Enoch was translated into heaven because he had pleased God through faith (vv. 4–6). The lesson for us is that God cannot be pleased outside of faith. The one who comes to God must believe that he *exists*, and that he is *good*. The one who comes to him this way is coming in the same way, and with the same confidence, as our ancient fathers.

Noah is another example. "By faith Noah, being warned by God concerning events as yet unseen, in reverent fear . . ." (v. 7). Noah was a wonderful man, and by his faith he condemned the antediluvian world. The flood is marked in the memory of the entire human race. This one is more than a Bible story, it is a story that anthropologists have found everywhere—from Greece to China, from the Babylonians to the North American Indians. Just like the geologists, everywhere they go, they run into evidence of a massive, *local* flood. Add them all up, and you might get warm.

Father Abraham saw nothing with his eyes (vv. 8–12). He did not know where he was going, but went anyway, trusting God. He lived as an alien in the land of promise. The author of Hebrews tells us that Abraham was looking far beyond an inherited territory. His wonderful wife Sarah looked far beyond a mere physical seed—she saw *you*, here by faith reading this book. The basis of her faith is judging him faithful who made the promise (v. 11). And the world is still filling with her descendants.

In case there could be any mistake, the author of Hebrews prevents us from saying that our spiritual ancestors dealt in temporal things while we Christians deal in spiritual things (vv. 13–16). They were not looking for an earthly reward; their interest, like ours, was the heavenly country. God is not ashamed to be their God, and they will come into the same heavenly city which God has built for all of us.

The patriarchs of Israel are our fathers. The Scriptures give us a noble lineage—Abraham, Isaac, Jacob, and Joseph. Abraham was willing to sacrifice Isaac, the one who carried the promise. Isaac blessed his sons concerning the future. Jacob blessed his grandsons. And Joseph made sure his bones were carried out of Egypt when Moses led the people free (vv. 17–22).

Then we come to our fellow Christian Moses, our brother Moses. Faith protected Moses at his birth (v. 23). Faith led Moses to leave the riches of Egypt in order to become a Christian (vv. 24–25). By faith he conquered Egypt, kept the Passover, and led the people of Israel free (vv. 27–29).

Joshua conquered Jericho by faith, and Rahab betrayed Jericho through that same faith (vv. 30–31).

There were numerous others of whom the world was not worthy (v. 38). But we don't have time to speak of them all—so read your Bibles (vv. 32–40). And learn the lesson. Although they had a good testimony, God delayed their reception of the promise—so that you could walk into the City with them, and not behind them (v. 40).

15

DISCIPLINE AND PUNISHMENT

The previous chapter, that great hall of fame, sets the stage for this particular exhortation. The author of Hebrews was not telling Bible stories to no purpose or end. He was emphasizing the centrality of faith in all previous trials because his readers needed an exhortation to persevere in *their* faith, in the midst of their trial and temptation. Remember the phrase from the previous chapter—"*became* victorious in battle."

> Therefore, since we are surrounded by so great a cloud of witnesses. . . . (Heb. 12:1–17)

This is a reference to what has just gone before. But the point of chapter eleven was not to get us to look at "the people of old" only. Rather, we are to observe them so that we might learn to look at what *they* were looking at. As we saw clearly, they saw Christ. As we consider their faithful testimony, we should imitate them, setting aside every weight and every sin that hinders our race. And so we should look to Jesus. He went through horrendous trials, keeping his eye on the joy that was coming (vv. 1–2), the joy that was set before him.

One of the things we must do is to understand our own trials in their right proportions. Our trials are usually not as bad as we think. Everyone thinks that no one else knows "what it is like," but put your trials in perspective. Think about what it was like for Christ, who endured great hostility from sinners. Furthermore, you are in the same position as the original recipients of this letter—you have not yet gone to the stake for your Lord (vv. 3–4). Most of us have not shed blood in our defense of the faith.

On top of all this, your trials *do* have an ordained purpose. They mark you out as one of God's children. Don't ever forget what the Scripture says: "My son, do not regard lightly the discipline of the Lord, nor be weary when reproved by him. For the Lord disciplines the one he loves, and chastises every son whom he receives." The word translated here as *chastises* could be rendered equally well as *flogs*. Some of God's favorites receive pretty rough treatment. Now if you endure chastening (v. 7), then you are demonstrating that it is in fact chastening. If you are without chastening, then you are a spiritual bastard (v. 8). This does not mean that a spiritual bastard is "without troubles." It means he is without teleological troubles—without *chastening*. His troubles appear to have no point. God disciplines his children, and there is a difference between discipline and punishment. Discipline is corrective; the point is to change something. Punishment is retributive; justice can be fully satisfied without the recipient of the punishment changing at all. But when a real son is disciplined, transformation also occurs.

Human fathers provide a dim example of the principle. The author of Hebrews does not suppose that the discipline administered by human fathers is a perfect example of God's discipline. We Christian fathers should have our discipline be as much like God's as possible, though even when the discipline is poor (men disciplining "as seemed best to them"), it still provides a spiritual lesson for us. If we respect sinners who administer discipline, how much more should we respect God, who is holy and has our ultimate holiness in mind? In neither case is the process fun. No discipline is pleasant at the time, but fix your eyes, as Jesus did, on the joy set before you (vv. 9–11).

So get up. Whenever a saint is being tempted to lose his faith, or walk away from it, the tendency is to retreat into his own little world, feeling sorry for himself. "*Nobody* knows what *this* is like." The Bible does not tell us that we are quite right, and that we have surpassed Job for trials. It tells us to get up, and stop whining. "Therefore lift your drooping hands and strengthen your weak knees, and make straight paths for your feet, so that what is lame may not be put out of joint but rather be healed" (vv. 12–13). And when you get up, your duties are right there in front of you. What are you to do with them?

First, pursue peace with all men (v. 14), then pursue holiness—no one sees the Lord without holiness (v. 14); reject the root of bitterness. It causes you to fall short of grace, and it defiles many others (v. 15). Do not fall into Esau's crass spiritual stupidity—profanity and fornication are extremely short-sighted, and the consequences will follow. A man reaps what he sows. Esau could not undo his selling of his birthright, although he sought that opportunity with tears.

Reverence and Godly Awe

As we worship God we must remember the glory of the covenant which enables us to worship him. Too many Christians regard the New Covenant as God "dumbing down" his requirements. The Old Testament represents graduate-school worship, and the New Testament somehow sends us all back for some training in the remedial basics. This thinking represents a gross distortion of biblical teaching. New Covenant worship is more mature than Old Covenant worship. This brings certain ramifications to mind. "For you have not come to what may be touched" (Heb. 12:18–29).

The people of Israel had been confronted with a terrible sight. When Israel gathered with Moses at the base of Sinai, they were confronted with a terrifying reality. The presence of God overwhelmed them in many ways—the fire on the mountain, the darkness and tempest, the trumpet, the voice of God, and the prohibition against coming to the mountain (vv. 18–20). Even Moses, considering the greatness of God and the sinfulness of the people, was afraid because of what was going on (v. 21).

The contrast is then made to the new mountain. We come to a great and awesome city. This passage contains a glorious description of the Christian church and her friends. The church is called the heavenly Mount Zion here, and is the city of the living God, that is, the heavenly Jerusalem (v. 22). We have come to an uncountable number of angels, gathered together with us. We have come to the Great Festival—the general assembly. The church of the firstborn is comprised of those registered in heaven. We have come to God himself, the perfect Judge, and we have come to the spirits of just men made perfect. Lastly, we have come to Christ and his sprinkled blood—blood that speaks of better things than Abel's blood did (vv. 23–24).

Now let us consider what the contrast means, the contrast between the old mountain and the new mountain. "See that you do not refuse him who is speaking . . ." (v. 25). Here is the point where modern Christians draw the lesson *down* when God speaks *up*. Our tendency is to assume that that the New Covenant is more user-friendly and tolerant of contempt displayed by the worshipper. This is precisely the *opposite* of what the Bible teaches. ". . . much less will we escape if we reject him who warns from heaven" (v. 25). Do not even *think* about turning away from the Lord of the Covenant. There were penalties for those who violated the law of Moses, but how much more *severe* will it be, our author says, for those who despise the word from heaven. It is hard to imagine how much clearer the New Testament could have been. The New Covenant contains sanctions, and they are more severe sanctions than the Mosaic law contained. There is really no way to account for this apart from the recent arguments put forward by *objective* covenant thinking.

This brings us to the heavenly shakedown. The author of Hebrews quotes from the second chapter of Haggai. Our pattern here should be the same in all examples of quotations from the Old Testament in the New. We must allow the New Testament to provide an inspired commentary on the passage from the Old. "For thus says the LORD of hosts: Yet once more, in a little while, I will shake the heavens and the earth and the sea and the dry land. And I will shake all nations, so that the treasures of all nations shall come in, and I will fill this house with glory, says the LORD of hosts. The silver is mine, and the gold is mine, declares the LORD of hosts. The latter glory of this house shall be greater than the former, says the LORD of hosts. And in this place I will give peace, declares the LORD of hosts" (Hag. 2:6–9).

The writer of Hebrews interprets this prophecy in this way. The giving of the covenant at Sinai brought a shaking of the earth. The New Covenant brings a shaking of the heavens as well. *This means* a shaking of all nations. When all nations are shaken, *they will come* to the Desire of All Nations, who is the Lord Jesus Christ. He is the one who brings in the kingdom which cannot be shaken. This is the kingdom of God, of which we are citizens. This is the kingdom which will grow and advance until it fills the earth. After the shaking, there is a kingdom which remains. The kingdom which remains is the kingdom of God. We as Christians are in the process of receiving this kingdom—as Jesus taught us to pray, "Your kingdom *come*, your will be done, on earth as it is in heaven . . ." He did not teach us to pray, "Your kingdom go, your will be done in heaven when we get there after we die . . ." In Daniel's vision this kingdom, which will last forever, struck the statue of the pagan king on the feet and destroyed them all. It grew to become a mountain that filled the earth. This kingdom can never be removed.

So the conclusion of the matter brings us to the importance of worship as the appointed means that God has assigned to bring about the manifestation of the Lord's kingdom. God is a consuming fire (v. 29). Our responsibility as New Covenant Christians is not to approach him with a breezy nonchalance. We must serve God *acceptably* (v. 28) with "reverence and awe" (v. 28). We are to worship God acceptably. This must mean that it is possible to worship him *unacceptably*. He may require blood sacrifice, and we are like Cain, showing up with the produce truck. The key note of this acceptable worship is reverence and godly fear. Worship must not be breezy and casual. The Bible says that it ought not to be. When we cultivate breezy and casual worship, we are retarding the growth of the kingdom.

One of the fundamental confusions of our era is that which muddles intimacy and informality. The Spirit does cause us to cry out *Abba, Father*, but the Spirit will never remove godly fear or awe because we always hallow his name.

A KINGDOM THAT CANNOT BE SHAKEN

As Christians, we live under the New Covenant. This is widely and mistakenly believed to be an indication of how God mellowed out between Malachi and Matthew. As we shall see, the mistake is a wild distortion of the Bible's teaching. "For I was afraid of the anger and hot displeasure that the LORD bore against you, so that he was ready to destroy you. But the LORD listened to me that time also" (Deut. 9:19). Moses is reminding the people of their rebelliousness throughout their time in the wilderness. During the course of his message to them, he recounted the fear he had over the sin of Israel. This comment is picked up by the author of Hebrews and placed in a (somewhat similar) message to Christians of the first century. The phrase is quoted in Hebrews 12:21.

The author of Hebrews gives us a strong contrast between the terrors that accompanied the giving of the law at Sinai and the godly fear that should motivate us now under the New Covenant. The contrast he sets begins in Hebrews 12:18 and continues on to verse 29, though the contrast is not what we might expect.

He begins by noting that Christians have not come to a *physical* mountain—a physical mountain where God appeared, causing terror among the people, and fear in Moses. They have come to a *heavenly* Mt. Zion. This is described in a number of additional ways. They have come to the city of the living God; the heavenly Jerusalem; an innumerable host of angels; to the general assembly—the church of the first born—all registered in heaven; to God the Judge of all; to the spirits of just men made perfect; to Jesus the Mediator of the New Covenant; to the sprinkled blood that speaks better than Abel.

This is the basis for New Covenant fear. Now the point of application is an *a fortiori* or "how much more" argument. The New

Covenant is not understood if we make it a means of saying that "God is now our buddy—not like in the *Old* Testament." We must note well the words of verse 25. "See that you do not refuse him who is speaking. For if they did not escape when they refused him who warned them on earth, *much less* will we escape if we reject him who warns from heaven."

What is going on? God is shaking down the kingdoms of men, so that which cannot be shaken—the kingdom of God—will remain. The conclusion of this line of argument is found in verses 28 and 29. The form of the argument is that if "you get the shakes before you appear in front of the governor, how much more will it happen when you appear before the president." Let us have grace, *by which* we may serve (that is, worship) God acceptably. There are two characteristics of such acceptable service: reverence and godly fear. Why? While the mountains have changed, God has *not*. Grace—and an understanding of grace—*increases* this right kind of fear.

RENEWED WEEKLY

One of the foundational assumptions beneath most modern Bible reading is the assumption of individualism. For example, Paul wrote the book of Ephesians to a *church*, but countless quiet times have taught us all to regard it as "a message for *me*." "How should *I* behave today? What should *I* do tomorrow?" Instead of seeing Scripture as a most holy collection of the church's covenant documents, we tend to see it as a grab bag of inspirational quotes for personal victorious living. Every man for himself, and devil take the hindmost.

It is important to note that a corporate covenantal understanding of Scripture does not exclude personal faithfulness; rather, it requires it. It is not possible to make a good omelet with rotten eggs, and so nothing written here can be taken as a disparagement of personal faithfulness. In contrast, an individualistic approach does not require corporate faithfulness. All the eggs in the world do not necessitate that someone make an omelet. In most cases, such individualism is sustained by a deliberate, cultivated low view of the institutional church, and this is radically unscriptural.

This question of individualism is important when we discuss what the Bible teaches about the public worship of God. This is because we have trained ourselves to miss the setting in which many well-known verses appear. When this corporate covenantal setting is taken into account, the testimony of Scripture is clear from beginning to end. God teaches us that public worship is *greatly* to be preferred to private spiritual exercises. "The LORD loves the gates of Zion more than all the dwelling places of Jacob. Glorious things of you are spoken, O city of God" (Ps. 87:2–3). Every grateful heart wants God's name to be lifted up publicly—and the more public the better. "Declare his glory among the nations, his marvelous works among all the peoples!" (Ps. 96:3). One of the most natural things for us as believers to do is congregate so that we might worship God *together.* "Oh come, let *us* worship and bow down; let *us* kneel before the LORD, our Maker!" (Ps. 95:6). "Oh, magnify the LORD with me, and *let us exalt his name together*!" (Ps. 34:3). Worship therefore belongs primarily in the congregation. "I will tell of your name to my brothers; in the midst *of the congregation* I will praise you . . . from you comes my praise *in the great congregation*; my vows I will perform before those who fear him" (Ps. 22:22, 25). Asaph struggled greatly in his private meditations—but when he finally went to the sanctuary God taught him (Ps. 73:16).

After his conquest of the principalities and powers, Christ followed the ancient custom where triumphant kings and generals scattered treasures among the people, and the result was that he gave gifts to men. He gave these gifts so that his church would be built up into "a perfect man." In order to accomplish this very public goal, he gave public officers, establishing them in the church (Eph. 4:11–14). The early Christians were filled with the Holy Spirit when they were assembled *together* (Acts 4:31). The tabernacles of the Lord are always appealing to the forgiven (Ps. 84:1). A day in God's courts is better than a thousand elsewhere (Ps. 84:10), and yet God in his kindness permits us to assemble there every *seventh* day (Lev. 23:3). The man who believes this while trusting God is truly blessed (Ps. 84:12). What one thing does the godly man want? That he might *dwell* in the house of God (Ps. 27:4). This is no fossilized relic of the forms of worship in the Old Testament. The day will come, the prophet said, when the inhabitant of one city will drag his brother off to worship God—and "I myself am going" (Zech. 8:20–21).

Christians have the enormous privilege of ascending into heaven in their worship on the Lord's Day. This *anaphora*, this lifting up, is what happens when the call to worship is given. When John was in the spirit on the Lord's Day (Rev. 1:10), he was caught up into the heavenly places. The same thing happens to us—on the first day of every week. "And the smoke of the incense, with the prayers of the saints, rose before God from the hand of the angel" (Rev. 8:4).

Paul tells the Ephesians that they were located in two places. The first was obvious—Ephesus (Eph. 1:1). But their second location is something he emphasizes strongly throughout the book. They are *in Christ*, who is in turn at the right hand of God the Father *in heaven*.

According to Paul, we were co-crucified with Christ, co-resurrected, and co-enthroned "in the heavenly places in Christ Jesus" (Eph. 2:5–6). We read these passages, but we individualize them. We go off to heaven in our private prayers, and rarely wonder where everyone else is.

Why should we not forsake the gathering of ourselves *together* (Heb. 10:25)? Too often this verse is quoted as simply meaning that a man should "go to church." It means this, of course, but neglects the riches involved when we go to church with a scriptural heart and mind. This is really a command to not neglect going to *heaven* in worship. The preceding context makes this abundantly clear. We have boldness to enter the Holy of Holies in heaven (10:19). How holy must *that* sanctuary be? Because we have this boldness, let *us* draw near with true hearts (10:22). When do we do this? On the sabbath rest that remains for the people of God (4:9), which is to say, on the Lord's Day. God created the heavens and earth in six days, and he hallowed the seventh day as one of holy rest. No sufficient reason for changing the day can be found—short of a new heavens and a new earth, in which righteousness dwells. We have a new sabbath because we have a new creation; the old has passed away. This is just what we find. Jesus Christ rested after his glorious work of re-creation, just as God had rested after the work of creation (4:10). This is why we still have a sabbath, and why we have the privilege of entering into a glorious heavenly rest.

In our public worship, we do not come to a mountain that can be touched (12:18), but we *do* come to a mountain, a heavenly Zion. What happens when a small group of saints gathers in a clapboard community church somewhere out in the sticks? At their call to worship, they ascend to the City of God, to the heavenly Jerusalem. They walk into the midst of innumerable angels (12:22). They come to the general assembly of the universal church, and come into the presence of God himself (12:23). Scripture says this understanding should rattle us—we should start working out our salvation together with fear and trembling (Phil. 2:12–13). When we understand what is actually happening in a worship service, our contemporary flippancy evaporates. Since we are receiving a kingdom that cannot be shaken, we are to have grace, so that *we* can worship with reverence and godly fear (12:28).

This godly fear should lead us to inquire how God wants us to approach him. What are the elements of our worship service as we renew our covenant with God weekly? First a word about this word *renewal*, which might be misunderstood. We do not renew our covenant with God because it was going to expire or run out, like a lease. We renew our covenant with God because it is our life; we renew covenant with God in worship the way food renews physical life or sexual communion renews marriage.

In the Old Testament, the sacrifices assigned by God had a particular order and placement—for an important reason. There were three offerings that were commonly found together, and when they were found together, they always followed a particular order (Lev. 9; 2 Chron. 29:20–36). First was the guilt offering (Lev. 17). Following this was the ascension offering, often misleadingly translated as burnt offering (Lev. 16:24–25). And third was the peace offering (Deut. 12:17–19). The guilt offering made the worshipper fit to enter into the presence of God. In the second offering, the worshipper ascended to God in the smoke of an offering that was entirely consumed on the altar. The peace offering was a tangible demonstration that God had received the worshipper, and was willing to share fellowship with him in common meal.

We know, of course, that in the New Testament, the sacrifices of animals are done away with in the once-for-all sacrifice of Christ on the cross (Heb. 9:12). But the language of these Old Testament sacrifices does *not* disappear. Rather, sacrificial patterns undergird all New Covenant worship. This is why we can understand the Bible as giving us a pattern of approach. First in the service, we confess our sins, which corresponds to the guilt offering. Then we offer ourselves up to God, without reserve or reluctance, which corresponds to the ascension offering. Then we sit down with God in the Lord's Supper, which corresponds to the peace offering. The heart of the service is bookended, at the beginning by the call to worship, and at the conclusion by the benediction, a commissioning that sends the people of God out into the world to serve him there (Rom. 12:1–2).

There are various legitimate ways in which this can be expressed, but here is a sample of how it could go. First is the *call* to worship, which includes a prayer of adoration and a congregational singing of *Gloria in excelsis*. Then is the element of *confession*, which includes an exhortation and a prayer of confession, assurance of pardon, and congregational singing of thanks. Next is the time of *consecration*. This includes the public reading of Scripture, the congregational time of prayer (petitions and thanks), the sermon, and a hymn or psalm of thanks. This time concludes with the offering brought forward in worship. Then is the time of *communion*, where the Lord's Supper is observed. Last is the *commissioning*, where the people sing the *Gloria Patri* with hands upraised, receive a final charge, and the benediction. God's promise is true, as always. "I am the LORD your God, who brought you up out of the land of Egypt. Open your mouth wide, and I will fill it" (Ps. 81:10).

All of this is glorious—why would anyone ever want to do anything else? "I was glad when they said to me, 'Let us go to the house of the LORD' " (Ps. 122:1). The answer is that we live in a fallen world. It is far easier to let the garden fill up with weeds than to cultivate and tend it. A basic principle laid down by God holds true in worship, just as it does everywhere else. A man's "slack hand causes poverty, but the hand of the diligent makes rich" (Prov. 10:4). Our contemporary worship is threadbare because we are lazy, and do not want to take the effort to study what God says about how we are to approach him. Among other things, all of them animated with faith, we are to approach him *diligently*. He "rewards those who seek him" (Heb. 11:6). The reformation of the church requires liturgical reformation, and our need is desperate. But when "the LORD builds up Zion, he appears in his glory" (Ps. 102:16).

We do not have fewer privileges than our brothers in the Old Testament did. Our place of worship is still "beautiful in elevation," "the joy of all the earth" (Ps. 48:2). This is only true if we do this understanding the character of God. We think of his lovingkindness—but we do it in the midst of his temple (Ps. 48:9).

APPLICATIONS FROM HEBREWS

As we conclude the book of Hebrews, the writer ends his letter with a potpourri of ethical admonitions and instruction. A common theme is "living in a certain way," but the subject matter changes radically from passage to passage. "Let brotherly love continue. . . ." (Heb. 13:1–25).

We begin with friends, strangers and prisoners. These believers are exhorted, as we are, to remember three classes of people. The first is made up of our brothers and sisters in the faith. The second is strangers—showing hospitality. The third is made up of prisoners who have been mistreated for the faith (vv. 1–3). Of course these prisoners are also members of the first category mentioned, but mentioning them particularly is still important. Many are attracted to the love of vibrant Christian communities, and do not mind joining up and joining in with the general pleasantness. But when trouble arises, and some members of that community run afoul of "respectable" authority, the situation changes. The apostle Paul even had to deal with this—visiting a subversive person in prison is a good way to get your own name on the blacklist. So, our writer tells us, don't back away from Christians who get in trouble with the law for their faith.

He then turns to discuss the marriage bed. The Christian faith is not at all an ascetic religion (v. 4). We are told in the plainest terms that marriage is honorable (this means, by the way, that it is to be *honored*), and the bed is undefiled. We should be far more concerned with sexual morality than with Victorian propriety. The two phrases *robust and lawful* and *prim and proper* are not interchangeable.

Keeping the marriage bed undefiled is closely related to the question of contentment. Discontentment begins with wanting other people's stuff—whether car, house, wife, children or money. Obedience to the tenth commandment is the fountainhead of contentment. Be content with what you have (v. 5). Whatever it is you are missing, God is there with you (vv. 5–6). While discontentment is a problem in every area, it is discontentment on fire (lust) that really causes trouble. God will judge adulterers and whoremongers, as we have just learned, and the key to staying out of that trouble is to learn the secret of *contentment*.

We then come to the important subject of church government. We see in these verses the New Testament requirement of church membership (vv. 7, 17, 24). Notice what the members of the church must do with regard to their elders—remember their teaching, imitate their faith, reflect on their behavior, obey them, and be a joy to them. The rulers must render an account. This cannot happen with the haphazard approach we have to church membership that is so common in our day. At the same time, the letter is not written to the rulers (v. 24). The saints are not simply ciphers, needing to be moved around by their elders.

This exhortation presupposes a knowledge of the rulers on the part of the members, and a knowledge of the members on the part of the rulers. It is not possible for an accountant to give an accounting unless he knows what he is dealing with. It is not possible for the elders of the church to give an accounting without church membership. Neither is it possible for the saints in the congregation to do what is required of them here without them knowing the names of the elders they are required to obey. Just try to imagine (for example) children being required to obey their parents without any knowledge of who their parents are. It is the same here. In order for Christians to obey their rulers, they must identify their rulers, and this means they need to know their names. In order for rulers to give an account for the congregation, they need to know their names. If you have any situation where there are two groups of people, known to each other, bound together by the covenantal obligations described here, you have a system of church membership. You do not have the free and breezy approach to church-hopping that is so characteristic of our times. This is because church membership is biblical, and flitting from fellowship to fellowship is not.

We then are reminded of the constancy of Christ. Christ never changes. Because he never changes, we should not be blown about by weird doctrines. We are to be built up by grace—we eat from God's altar by faith (vv. 8–10). This is an altar from which the Jews have no right to partake. As we gather around the Lord's Table weekly, we are nourished and strengthened. This does not place superstitious value on bread and wine any more than gathering to hear the word of Christ preached places superstitious faith in the paper and ink on the page of the Bible, or in the vocal cords of the preacher. God uses means, and these means are no blessing to us whatever unless we approach them in evangelical faith.

As we partake of Christ in this altar, we come to bear his reproach. The sacrificial animals of the Old Covenant were taken outside the camp. When Christ came, he died outside the city. In the same way, we should be willing to take our place with him *outside* the camp (vv. 11–14). If God wills, we must be willing to share the contempt placed upon him. Returning to the earlier exhortation, this is part of the reason we should remember those Christians who were imprisoned for their faith. All those who desire to live a godly life in Christ Jesus will be persecuted. This is God's pattern, and we should never identify godliness with a mere middle-class respectability.

The Christian faith consists of offering up sacrifices. We don't offer animals any more, for the ultimate Sacrifice has come, and offered himself up once for all. Our worship is still sacrificial worship, and follows the patterns of sacrificial worship set down in the Old Testament. Two sacrifices form part of our life before God. The first is the sacrifice of praise—this is to be a continuous sacrifice (v. 15). This is only possible when rendered as fruit (v. 15). The second sacrifice is that of good works and sharing (v. 16). God is pleased when we share our lives with one another. New Covenant worship is sacrificial worship that overflows as gratitude.

Then we come to a personal request. The author of Hebrews requests prayer, and does so on the basis of a good conscience (vv. 18–19). Never let the fact you cannot be absolutely faultless in God's sight make room for allowances with regard to honorable living. If God were to mark iniquities, no one could stand. It does not follow from this that blameless and honorable living is an impossibility. Much confusion is caused by confounding what our lives would look like in the sight of God (apart from Christ) and what they look like as we walk by faith in Christ in the sight of all men.

Another personal note comes in at verses 22 and 23. He begs their patience for the "few words" he has written, and he mentions the news about Timothy (v. 23).

We then come to the benediction and greeting. The God who did one thing (raise Jesus from the dead) can do another. He can make us complete in every good work to do his will—doing, again, what pleases him (vv. 20–25).

HE WILL NEVER LEAVE YOU

We come now to the very precious doctrine of the preservation and perseverance of the saints. This is based upon the faithfulness of God, and *not* the faithfulness of man. Because God is faithful, we can be. However, these saints are not gathered for a church picnic; they are a pilgrim *army*.

We should begin by reading through the first eight verses of Deuteronomy 31. This is part of Moses' final exhortation and encouragement before the invasion of Canaan. It is crucial to note the context. We are not considering a situation where someone is being told to "hang on because Friday's coming." It is the word spoken to an invading army about to go into combat. "Be strong and courageous. Do not fear or be in dread of them, for it is the LORD your

God who goes with you. He will not leave you or forsake you" (Deut. 31:6). This phrase is found twice in this passage, and it is repeated later for Joshua's encouragement. The application is found here in the thirteenth chapter of Hebrews.

We are reminded again of how Hebrews is a New Covenant Deuteronomy. The parallels are remarkable indeed. In each case, there has been a remarkable deliverance (2:14–16). In each case, the people received the Word of God (2:3). In each case, we find the formation of a people (3:5–6). In each case, the problem is possible apostasy (6:1–8). In each case, there is a coming invasion (2:5). We see in Hebrews a self-conscious comparison (3:7–4:13). We must consider the time involved—about forty years between each exodus and each invasion. Remember, of course, the placement of the book—each book is a word of final exhortation before battle.

This is preparation for godly fighting. Remembering that we are receiving a kingdom which cannot be shaken (12:28), the author of Hebrews gives a series of exhortations for this warfare. We are to maintain a continuing brotherly love. Nothing is worse than an army fighting itself (v. 1). Be hospitable; in doing so, do not forget that appearances can be deceiving (v. 2). Identify with casualties. Those persecuted and mistreated should be remembered by you (v. 3). Honor the marriage bed, and the covenantal oaths surrounding it (v. 4). Resist covetousness (v. 5). Resist discontentment (v. 5).

If the camp of the army is clean, the Lord will travel with it, and bless it. If there is sin in the camp, if there is tolerated evil, if there is murmuring or avarice, if there is sexual uncleanness, if there is bickering, if there is inhospitable selfishness, if there is thoughtlessness for those wounded, the Lord will not bless that army in the field. Conversely, if the army is prepared for the Lord in the midst of the camp, then no one can stand before it.

APPENDIX A

AUTHORSHIP OF HEBREWS

THE LETTER OF PAUL TO THE HEBREWS

Throughout this book, I have referred variously to the "writer of Hebrews" and the "author of Hebrews," along with other circumlocutions. I did not do this because I have no convictions about the authorship of the letter, but rather because the view I hold is somewhat out of fashion, and I did not want to invite the average reader to begin looking at this book with a jaundiced eye. Normally, commentaries on a book of the Bible begin with the authorship question, and I did not follow this quite reasonable pattern simply because I did not want to prejudice the reader. Now that the book has probably been read, and the damage largely done, we can afford to raise the question of its authorship.

With all this said, I hold that the letter was written by the apostle Paul. Many other suggestions have been offered in the history of the church. Luther held that it was written by Apollos—quite a reasonable suggestion when you consider that Apollos was eloquent and mighty in the Scriptures (Acts 18:24), a description that certainly fits the writer of this book. Origen mentions that some attributed it to Luke. Some have suggested Clement of Rome, and others like Tertullian have put Barnabas forward. But the reason it was included in the canon of Scripture is that the consensus of the ancient church was that it was written by Paul. My copy of the King James Bible entitles the letter "The Epistle of Paul the Apostle to the Hebrews." To others, influenced by modern textual study, this attribution has the same level of authority as do the maps and the concordance.

In what follows, I am indebted to the work of the great Puritan theologian John Owen (John Owen, *The Works of John Owen, Vol. 17*, 65–95), and I simply intend to summarize and represent his central arguments, those which I found compelling. Those who want to pursue this question in greater detail can find more than enough material in Owen on it. His commentary on Hebrews runs to seven volumes, with the first two volumes constituting the introduction.

While the church is not settled at all on the authorship of this book, the modern consensus against the Pauline argument is that "it doesn't sound like him," or, as John Owen put it, "dissimilitude of style." This was an objection that the ancients knew and understood, and they attributed it to Paul anyway. The book of Hebrews is written in elegant Greek, and the apostle Paul confessed himself to be "unskilled in speaking" (2 Cor. 11:6).

There are three ways to answer this objection without dropping the Pauline authorship. The first is to say that Paul wrote the letter to the Hebrews *in* Hebrew, and that it was subsequently translated and polished up by someone else. A second possibility would be the lecture or sermon notes thesis. In this view, Paul preached this as a sermon, and notes were taken down by an educated auditor, who then edited the notes for publication. A third possibility, the one I prefer, is that Paul's self-deprecatory description of his own rhetorical abilities ought not to be pressed too far. In conjunction with this, Paul (like other men of genius) was quite capable of writing in different settings and for different occasions. All of his other letters are occasional letters, written by him in his role as the apostle to the Gentiles. Many of them bear the marks of having been written in haste, or in response to a crisis (as in Galatia). This letter is addressed to Hebrew Christians, and we have every reason to believe that the situation called for a different approach than what Paul usually did. Paul was not an illiterate hedge preacher, unable to function once you got him off his talking points. He was one of the greatest men who ever lived—in zeal, in ability, in wisdom, in love, in scholarship, and in understanding—and was a genius of the first order. If we turn the question around, and ask if a letter as accomplished as the letter to the Hebrews was beyond Paul's abilities, the question should answer itself. Of course it was not. The whole thing depends upon context and opportunity.

Samuel Rutherford, writing to a woman who had lost her daughter in death, said this: "But what! do you think her lost, when she is but sleeping in the bosom of the Almighty? Think her not absent who is in such a friend's house. Is she lost to you who is found to Christ? If she were with a dear friend, although you should never see her again, your care for her would be but small. Oh now, is she not with a dear friend, and gone higher." [Samuel Rutherford, *Letters of Samuel Rutherford* (Carlisle, PA: Banner of Truth, 1973), 14].

Rutherford also wrote this: "That power which is obliged to command and rule justly and religiously for the good of the subjects, and is only set over the people on these conditions, and not absolutely, cannot tie the people to subjection without resistance, when the power is abused to the destruction of laws, religion, and the subjects. But all power of the law is thus obliged" [Samuel Rutherford, *Lex Rex* (http://www.apuritansmind.com/Samuel Rutherford/SamuelRutherfordLexRex.htm)].

Context changes a lot. An argument could be made that the author of Rutherford's Letters could not possibly been the same man who wrote *Lex Rex*. So when you are dealing with someone with Paul's abilities and understanding, and when that is coupled with a completely different setting, there is no reason to suppose that he would be unequal to the task. These are simply answers to objections.

The first positive argument is taken from the testimony of the apostle Peter. The short form of this argument is that Paul wrote Hebrews because Peter says (in effect) that Paul did. "And count the patience of our Lord as salvation, just as our beloved brother Paul also *wrote to you* according to the wisdom given him, as he does in all his letters when he speaks in them of these matters. There are some things in them that are hard to understand, which the ignorant and unstable twist to their own destruction, as they do the other Scriptures" (2 Pet. 3:15–16).

The italicized words are *written to you*. Peter is saying that Paul wrote a letter to the same group of people that the second epistle of Peter was written to. And who was that? According to 2 Peter 3:1, Peter was writing his second epistle to this group, our letter of 1 Peter being the first. And who was addressed in that letter? The answer is the "elect exiles of the dispersion in Pontus, Galatia, Cappadocia, Asia, and Bithynia" (1 Pet. 1:1). James addresses the same group, addressing the "twelve tribes in the Dispersion" (Jas. 1:1). James and Peter were both apostles to the Circumcision, and this is plainly reflected in their letters. The *diaspora* was the scattering of Jews throughout the Gentile world, and this *diaspora* was also something that writers addressing Christian Jews would use. This argument means that Peter says, in 2 Peter, *that Paul had written to this same group*. In addition to all his other letters, Peter says, Paul has also written one *to you*. But what letter of Paul's would fit this description? Hebrews. As Owen notes, pointedly, we can't get off the point by saying that the letter that Peter is referring to got lost. "To affirm that the church hath lost an epistle to the Hebrews by St. Paul, and taken up one in the room thereof, written by, no man knoweth whom" (85).

In addition, Peter marks that the letter written by Paul to them was a letter marked by a particular *wisdom*. This letter stands out. That did not make it easy to follow—Peter mentions that Paul was sometimes hard to understand, and the letter to the Hebrews makes a very similar point (Heb. 5:11).

A second positive argument for the Pauline authorship of this letter is the testimony of the ancient church. The Western church had doubts and questions about it, but the Eastern church was clear on the point, and the Eastern church had advantages over the Western church in this matter, because they were in first possession of the letter. Their arguments were obviously persuasive to the westerners because they accepted it into the canon, but it is important to note that they accepted it into the canon *as the work of Paul*. Had the ancient church been convinced that "nobody knows who wrote this thing," that would have been an argument for rejecting the book.

Appendix B

Old Testament Quotations in Hebrews

"When your days are fulfilled and you lie down with your fathers, I will raise up your offspring after you, who shall come from your body, and I will establish his kingdom. He shall build a house for my name, and I will establish the throne of his kingdom forever. **I will be to him a father, and he shall be to me a son.** When he commits iniquity, I will discipline him with the rod of men, with the stripes of the sons of men, but my steadfast love will not depart from him, as I took it from Saul, whom I put away from before you. And your house and your kingdom shall be made sure forever before me. Your throne shall be established forever." In accordance with all these words, and in accordance with all this vision, Nathan spoke to David. (2 Sam. 7:12–17)

Or again, "**I will be to him a father, and he shall be to me a son**"? (Heb. 1:5b)

This is a promise given to the entire Davidic line, the line that culminates with Christ. This means that some of it is not directly applicable to Jesus ("When he commits iniquity . . ."), but nevertheless the passage is authoritatively applied to him.

"And **let all the sons of God worship him.**" (Deut. 32:43, LXX)

"Confounded be all they that serve graven images, that boast themselves of idols: **worship him, all ye gods**" (Ps. 97:7), "all his angels" in the LXX.

And again, when he brings the firstborn into the world, he says, "**Let all God's angels worship him.**" (Heb. 1:6)

The gods of the old aeon were commanded to worship the Messiah. We see here that these gods were angels—whether fallen or unfallen.

"Bless the LORD, O my soul! O LORD my God, you are very great! You are clothed with splendor and majesty, covering yourself with light as with a garment, stretching out the heavens like a tent. He lays the beams of his chambers on the waters; he makes the clouds his chariot; he rides on the wings of the wind; **he makes his messengers winds, his ministers a flaming fire**. He set the earth on its foundations, so that it should never be moved (Ps. 104:1–5).

"**Who maketh his angels winds . . .**" (Ps. 103:4, LXX)

Of the angels he says, "**He makes his angels winds, and his ministers a flame of fire**" (Heb. 1:7).

Lest the reader be thrown off here, the numbering of the psalms differs in the Septuagint. It is referring to the same psalm.

My heart overflows with a pleasing theme; I address my verses to the king; my tongue is like the pen of a ready scribe. You are the most handsome of the sons of men; grace is poured upon your lips; therefore God has blessed

But of the Son he says, "**Your throne, O God, is forever and ever, the scepter of uprightness is the scepter of your kingdom. You have loved righteousness and hated wickedness; there-**

you forever. Gird your sword on your thigh, O mighty one, in your splendor and majesty! In your majesty ride out victoriously for the cause of truth and meekness and righteousness; let your right hand teach you awesome deeds! Your arrows are sharp in the heart of the king's enemies; the peoples fall under you. **Your throne, O God, is forever and ever. The scepter of your kingdom is a scepter of uprightness; you have loved righteousness and hated wickedness. Therefore God, your God, has anointed you with the oil of gladness beyond your companions.** (Ps. 45:1–7)

fore God, your God, has anointed you with the oil of gladness beyond your companions" (Heb. 1:8–9).

God is speaking to the Son, and he addresses him as God. The psalm is a wedding psalm, and so we should see more than simply the coronation of Christ as king, we should also see the crowning of his bride—the church.

"O my God," I say, "take me not away in the midst of my days—you whose years endure throughout all generations!" **Of old you laid the foundation of the earth, and the heavens are the work of your hands. They will perish, but you will remain; they will all wear out like a garment. You will change them like a robe, and they will pass away, but you are the same, and your years have no end**. The children of your servants shall dwell secure; their offspring shall be established before you. (Ps. 102:24–28)

And, "You, Lord, **laid the foundation of the earth in the beginning, and the heavens are the work of your hands; they will perish, but you remain; they will all wear out like a garment, like a robe you will roll them up, like a garment they will be changed. But you are the same, and your years will have no end.**" (Heb. 1:10–12)

The Lord is spoken of here as the Creator of all things. He is the one who laid the foundations of the earth, and he is the one who sustains it. The author of Hebrews clearly identifies Jesus as the Creator God.

The LORD says to my Lord: "**Sit at my right hand, until I make your enemies your footstool.**" (Ps. 110:1)

And to which of the angels has he ever said, "**Sit at my right hand until I make your enemies a footstool for your feet**"? (Heb. 1:13)

This was referenced above, as we noted.

When I look at your heavens, the work of your fingers, the moon and the stars, which you have set in place, **what is man that you are mindful of him, and the son of man that you care for him? Yet you have made him a little lower than the heavenly beings and crowned him with glory and honor. You have given him dominion over the works of your hands; you have put all things under his feet**, all sheep and oxen, and also the beasts of the field, the birds of the heavens, and the fish of the sea, whatever passes along the paths of the seas. O LORD, our Lord, how majestic is your name in all the earth! (Ps. 8:3–9)

It has been testified somewhere, "**What is man, that you are mindful of him, or the son of man, that you care for him? You made him for a little while lower than the angels; you have crowned him with glory and honor, putting everything in subjection under his feet.**" (Heb. 2:6–8a)

In principle man was given dominion over everything, and this astonished David. At the same time, the fullness of this promise had clearly not come to pass—until Christ.

I will tell of your name to my brothers; in the midst of the congregation I will praise you. (Ps. 22:22)

For he who sanctifies and those who are sanctified all have one source. That is why he is not ashamed to call them brothers, saying, "**I will tell of your name to my brothers; in the midst of the congregation I will sing your praise.**" (Heb. 2:11–12)

The point of this citation is to show that Christ is not ashamed to call us his brothers. But we also see in passing that Christ is identifying with his brothers after his resurrection. Recall that the first part of Psalm 22 is the famous prophecy of the crucifixion, and this statement of praise occurs after that.

Bind up the testimony; seal the teaching among my disciples. I will wait for the LORD, who is hiding his face from the house of Jacob, and **I will hope in him** (Is. 8:16–17; "**I will put my trust in him**" for "I will look for him," LXX).

And again, "**I will put my trust in him.**" (Heb. 2:13a)

Putting trust in God is expressed here in the context of waiting upon the Lord, looking for him. And of course, the message of Hebrews is that the Messiah has now come and has been established at the right hand of God. The one in whom we trusted, and for whom we looked, has arrived.

Behold, **I and the children whom the LORD has given me** are signs and portents in Israel from the LORD of hosts, who dwells on Mount Zion. (Is. 8:18)

And again, "Behold**, I and the children God has given me.**" (Heb. 2:13b)

The point here is not just that God has given Christ "children," but also that he gave these children to Christ *to be a sign and wonder* in Israel. The citizens of the new Israel were a testimony to the citizens of the old Israel.

But you, Israel, my servant, Jacob, whom I have chosen, **the offspring of Abraham, my friend; you whom I took** from the ends of the earth, and called from its farthest corners, saying to you, "You are my servant,

For surely it is not angels that he helps, **but he helps the offspring of Abraham.** (Heb. 2:16)

I have chosen you and not cast you off." (Is. 41:8–9)

The Messiah did not become an angel; he did not take on himself the nature of angels. Rather, he took hold of the seed of Abraham, meaning that he took *on* the nature of Abraham's seed.

I will tell of your name **to my brothers**; in the midst of the congregation I will praise you. (Ps. 22:22)

Therefore he had to be made **like his brothers** in every respect, so that he might become a merciful and faithful high priest in the service of God, to make propitiation for the sins of the people. (Heb. 2:17)

Because he became a man, Christ has been placed in a number of family relationships. He has been given children (remember that Isaiah calls him "Everlasting Father"); he has become a child (he has taken on the nature of the *seed* of Abraham); and here he is placed as the eldest brother among many brethren.

For he is our God, and we are the people of his pasture, and the sheep of his hand. **Today, if you hear his voice, do not harden your hearts, as at Meribah, as on the day at Massah in the wilderness, when your fathers put me to the test and put me to the proof, though they had seen my work. For forty years I loathed that generation and said, "They are a people who go astray in their heart, and they have not known my ways." Therefore I swore in my wrath, "They shall not enter my rest."** (Ps. 95:7–11)

Therefore, as the Holy Spirit says, "**Today, if you hear his voice, do not harden your hearts as in the rebellion, on the day of testing in the wilderness, where your fathers put me to the test and saw my works for forty years. Therefore I was provoked with that generation, and said, 'They always go astray in their heart; they have not known my ways.' As I swore in my wrath, 'They shall not enter my rest.'** " Take care, brothers, lest there be in any of you an evil, unbelieving heart, leading you to fall away from the living God. But exhort one another every day, as long as it is called "today," that none of you may be hardened by the deceitfulness of sin. For we have come to share in Christ, if indeed we hold our original confidence firm to the end. As it is said, "Today, if you hear his voice, do not harden your hearts as in the rebellion." For who were those who heard and yet rebelled? Was it not all those who left Egypt led by Moses? And with whom was he provoked for forty years? Was it not with those who sinned, whose bodies fell in the wilderness? And to whom did he swear that they would not enter his rest, but to those who were disobedient? So we see that they were unable to enter because of unbelief. (Heb. 3:7–19)

The warnings of Psalm 95 form a key part of the argument in the book of Hebrews. Just as the Jews in the wilderness were being tested, so the first generation of Christians was being tested *in the same way*.

Therefore I swore in my wrath, "They shall not enter my rest." (Ps. 95:11)

Therefore, while the promise of entering his rest still stands, let us fear lest any of you should seem to have failed to reach it. For good news came to us just as to them, but the message they heard did not benefit them, because they were not united by faith with those who listened. For we who have believed enter that rest, as he has said, "**As I swore in my wrath, 'They shall not enter my rest**,' " although his works were finished from the foundation of the world." (Heb. 4:1–3)

Moses spoke to a mixed multitude, all of whom had been destined to deliverance from Egypt, but not all of whom were destined to enter the promised land. The writer to the Hebrews has the same situation before him. Deliverance from slavery and entry into rest are not the same thing.

Thus the heavens and the earth were finished, and all the host of them. And on the seventh day God finished his work that he had done, **and he rested on the seventh day from all his work that he had done**. So God blessed the seventh day and made it holy, because on it God rested from all his work that he had done in creation. (Gen. 2:1–3)

For he has somewhere spoken of the seventh day in this way: "**And God rested on the seventh day from all his works.**" (Heb. 4:4)

Up to this point, the rest that the writer to the Hebrews commends is compared to the rest of the land of Canaan. Now he shifts to a different image—the rest that God took on the completion of the creation week—sabbath rest.

Therefore I swore in my wrath, "**They shall not enter my rest.**" (Ps. 95:11)

And again in this passage he said, "They shall not **enter my rest**." Since therefore it remains for some to enter it, and those who formerly received the good news **failed to enter** because of disobedience. (Heb. 4:5–6)

The fact that God swore that some of the Jews in the wilderness would not enter his rest meant that they had not already entered it. Those who entered the Canaan rest were able to do so because of their faith, and those who died in the wilderness did so because of unbelief. They had been freed from the bondage of Egypt, but there was still more that had to be accomplished. The recipients of this letter had been delivered in an analogous way, and they had an analogous choice before them.

For he is our God, and we are the people of his pasture, and the sheep of his hand. **Today, if you hear his**

Again he appoints a certain day, "Today," saying through David so long afterward, in the words al-

voice, do not harden your hearts, as at Meribah, as on the day at Massah in the wilderness. (Ps. 95:7–8)

ready quoted, "**Today, if you hear his voice, do not harden your hearts.**" (Heb. 4:7)

The writer emphasizes the word *today*. The time for making this decision is now, not later. The Jews in the wilderness should have decided that day to hear the words of Moses. The Jews who first heard the words of Psalm 95 had an obligation to heed the words of God that day. And the Christians of the first century had the same duty. Should we listen to the voice of God? Well, is today *today*? If yes, then we should do what God says.

Thus the heavens and the earth were finished, and all the host of them. **And on the seventh day God finished his work that he had done**, and he rested on the seventh day from all his work that he had done. So God blessed the seventh day and made it holy, because on it God rested from all his work that he had done in creation. (Gen. 2:1–3)

For if Joshua had given them rest, God would not have spoken of another day later on. So then, there remains a Sabbath rest for the people of God, for whoever has entered God's rest has also **rested from his works as God did from his**. (Heb. 4:8–10)

The comparison is made to God's creation of the world. This means that the "he" who is ceasing from his own works is not ceasing from Pharisaical self-righteousness, which is not at all like God creating the world. Rather, the comparison is to Christ. Christ rested from his work of re-creating the world in just the same way that God rested from his work of creating the world in the first place. This is why a sabbath rest remains for the people of God—because they are the people of the new creation, and a new creation must have a new sabbath. God created the world in six days and six nights. Jesus re-created the heavens and earth, making a new heavens and a new earth in three days and three nights. When he rose from the dead on the first day of the week, resting from his work just as God had done from his, he sanctified the Lord's Day as a sabbath rest for the New Covenant people of God.

Therefore I swore in my wrath, "They shall not **enter my rest.**" (Ps. 95:11)

Let us therefore strive to **enter that rest**, so that no one may fall by the same sort of disobedience. (Heb. 4:11)

In both testaments, God speaks to his people—a mixed multitude containing both elect and non-elect individuals. He speaks to all of them, telling them to enter into his rest. The only sin that would prevent such entering is unbelief.

I will tell of the decree: The LORD said to me, "**You are my Son; today I have begotten you**. Ask of me, and I will make the nations your heritage, and the ends of the earth your possession. You shall break them with a rod of iron and dash them in pieces like a potter's vessel." (Ps. 2:7–9)

So also Christ did not exalt himself to be made a high priest, but was appointed by him who said to him, "**You are my Son, today I have begotten you.**" (Heb. 5:5)

As we have already noted, this is a reference to Christ being the firstborn from among the dead, and is not a reference to his eternal Sonship. That is taught elsewhere, but here we are being told that Christ was begotten from the dead in his resurrection, and that begetting was a declaration on God's part of his status as a Son. God declared him to be the Son of God, with power, by his resurrection (Rom. 1:4). Note also that immediately after his resurrection, the psalm shows him being invited to ask for the ends of the earth for his possession.

The LORD has sworn and will not change his mind, "**You are a priest forever after the order of Melchizedek.**" (Ps. 110:4)

As he says also in another place, "**You are a priest forever, after the order of Melchizedek.**" In the days of his flesh, Jesus offered up prayers and supplications, with loud cries and tears, to him who was able to save him from death, and he was heard because of his reverence. Although he was a son, he learned obedience through what he suffered. And being made perfect, he became the source of eternal salvation to all who obey him, being designated by God a high **priest after the order of Melchizedek.** (Heb. 5:6–10)

Psalm 110 is central to the development of the argument in Hebrews. The first part speaks of the Lord being invited to sit at God's right hand, a point which Hebrews points to in multiple places. At the end of the psalm, we see that the one who is invited to sit in the royal position of rule is also an eternal priest in the order of Melchizedek. This point is referred to again and again in Hebrews.

And God said, "**Let the earth sprout vegetation, plants yielding seed**, and fruit trees bearing fruit in which is their seed, each according to its kind, on the earth." And it was so. (Gen. 1:11)

For land that has drunk the rain that often falls on it, and **produces a crop** useful to those for whose sake it is cultivated, receives a blessing from God. (Heb. 6:7)

God gives his gifts for blessing, and he does so in both testaments. God extends grace, and disobedience is consistently a twisting of that grace.

And said, "**By myself I have sworn**, declares the LORD, because you have done this and have not withheld your son, your only son, **I will surely bless you, and I will surely multiply** your offspring as the stars of heaven and as the sand that is on the seashore. And your offspring shall possess the gate of his enemies." (Gen. 22:16–17)

For when God made a promise to Abraham, since he had no one greater by whom to swear, **he swore by himself, saying, "Surely I will bless you and multiply you."** (Heb. 6:13–14)

There is no authority above God to which he might appeal. He swears, when he swears, by himself. And on that authority, Abraham was assured that his descendants would be like the grains of sand on the seashore, and like the stars in the sky.

The Lord spoke to Moses after the death of the two sons of Aaron, when they drew near before the Lord and died, and the Lord said to Moses, "Tell Aaron your brother not **to come** at any time into the Holy Place **inside the veil**, before the mercy seat that is on the ark, so that he may not die. For I will appear in the cloud over the mercy seat." (Lev. 16:1–2)

[S]o that by two unchangeable things, in which it is impossible for God to lie, we . . . might have strong encouragement to hold fast to the hope set before us. We have this as a sure and steadfast anchor of the soul, a hope that **enters into the inner place behind the curtain**, where Jesus has gone as a forerunner on our behalf, having become a high priest forever after the order of Melchizedek. (Heb. 6:18–20)

The high priest would go into the Holy of Holies once a year, on the Day of Atonement. Having made atonement for the sins of the people, he would then come out again. Christ has entered the ultimate of Holy Places in the heavenlies, but he has not yet come out. When he does, this phase of our world's history will be over.

After his return from the defeat of Chedorlaomer and the kings who were with him, the king of Sodom went out to meet him at the Valley of Shaveh (that is, the King's Valley). And **Melchizedek** king of Salem brought out bread and wine. (He was priest of God Most High.) And he **blessed him** and said, "Blessed be Abram by God Most High, Possessor of heaven and earth; and blessed be God Most High, who has delivered your enemies into your hand!" **And Abram gave him a tenth of everything.** (Gen. 14:17–20)

For this **Melchizedek**, king of Salem, priest of the Most High God, met Abraham returning from the slaughter of the kings **and blessed him**, and to him **Abraham apportioned a tenth part of everything**. He is first, by translation of his name, king of righteousness, and then he is also king of Salem, that is, king of peace. He is without father or mother or genealogy, having neither beginning of days nor end of life, but resembling the Son of God he continues a priest forever. (Heb. 7:1–3)

Abraham paid tithes to Melchizedek, thus demonstrating the lines of spiritual authority. The lesser is blessed by the greater, and the lesser pays tithes to the greater. The writer to the Hebrews makes much of the relationship described between Abraham and Melchizedek. Note that Abraham gives the tithe to Melchizedek; Melchizedek gives Abraham a blessing, and gives him bread and wine.

And he blessed him and said, "Blessed be Abram by God Most High, Possessor of heaven and earth; and blessed be God Most High, who has delivered your enemies into your hand!" **And Abram gave him a tenth of everything.** (Gen. 14:19–20)

See how great this man was **to whom Abraham the patriarch gave a tenth of the spoils**! And those descendants of Levi who receive the priestly office have a commandment in the law to take tithes from the people, that is, from their brothers, though these also are descended from Abraham. But this man who does not have his descent from them received tithes from Abraham and blessed him who had the promises. It is beyond dispute that the inferior is blessed by the superior. In the one case tithes are received by mortal men, but in the other case, by one of whom it is testified that he lives. One might even say that Levi himself, who receives tithes, paid tithes through Abraham, for he was still in the loins of his ancestor when Melchizedek met him. (Heb. 7:4–10)

Here the argument is expressly made—Melchizedek had to be greater than Abraham because he was the recipient of the tithe. And because all Levites were descended from Abraham, this meant that in principle the Levitical priesthood was tithing to the Melchizedekan priesthood, thereby establishing that the latter was a greater priesthood. This is not just a flight of fancy—all of Israel tithed to the tribe of Levi, and the tribe of Levi tithed to the priests, who made up a subset of their tribe. In other words, lawful recipients of the tithe would tithe to the next level up.

The LORD has sworn and will not change his mind, "You are a priest forever after the order of Melchizedek." (Ps. 110:4)

Now if perfection had been attainable through the Levitical priesthood (for under it the people received the law), what further need would there have been for another priest to arise **after the order of Melchizedek,** rather than one named after the order of Aaron? For when there is a change in the priesthood, there is necessarily a change in the law as well. For the one of whom these things are spoken belonged to another tribe, from which no one has ever served at the altar. For it is evident that our Lord was descended from Judah, and in connection with that tribe Moses said nothing about priests. This becomes even more evident when another priest arises in the likeness of Melchizedek, who has become a priest, not on the basis of a legal requirement concerning bodily descent, but by the power of an indestructible life. For it is witnessed of him, "**You are a priest forever, after the order of Melchizedek**." For on the one hand, a former commandment is set aside because of its weakness and uselessness (for the law made nothing perfect); but on the other hand, a better hope is introduced, through which we draw near to God. And it was not without an oath. For those who formerly became priests were made such without an oath, but this one was made a priest with an oath by the one who said to him: "**The Lord has sworn and will not change his mind, You are a priest forever**." This makes Jesus the guarantor of a better covenant. The former priests were many in number, because they were prevented by death from continuing in office, but he holds his priesthood permanently, because he continues forever. Consequently, he is able to save to the uttermost those who draw near to God through him, since he always lives to make intercession for them. For it was indeed fitting that we should have such a high priest, holy, innocent, unstained, separated from sinners, and exalted above the heavens. He has no need, like those high priests, to offer sacrifices daily, first for his own sins and then for those of the people, since he did this once for all when he offered up himself. For the law appoints men in their weakness as high priests, but the word of the oath, which came later than the law, appoints a Son who has been made perfect forever. (Heb. 7:11–28)

The argument in Hebrews is not "after the fact" special pleading. A thousand years before Christ, the psalmist noted the uniqueness of Melchizedek, and a prophecy was given that said the Messiah would belong to that priesthood instead of the Levitical order.

The LORD says to my Lord: "**Sit at my right hand**, until I make your enemies your footstool." (Ps. 110:1)

Now the point in what we are saying is this: we have such a high priest, one who is **seated at the right hand** of the throne of the Majesty in heaven. (Heb. 8:1)

The same point is made yet again. This Melchizedekan priest is a royal priest (he was the king of Salem), and he is given the royal seat at the right hand of God.

How lovely are your tents, O Jacob, **your encampments**, O Israel! Like palm groves that stretch afar, like gardens beside a river, like aloes **that the LORD has planted**, like cedar trees beside the waters. (Num. 24:5–6)

Now the point in what we are saying is this: we have such a high priest, one who is seated at the right hand of the throne of the Majesty in heaven, a minister in the holy places, in the **true tent that the Lord set up**, not man. (Heb. 8:1–2)

In the Numbers passage, the planting which the Lord accomplishes is that of trees alongside the water. But in the previous verse, the tabernacles of Israel are mentioned, and so it appears that the author of Hebrews has taken this as a figure of speech—the planting of the trees as a figure of planting the tabernacles, and then the reference applied to the true tabernacle, the heavenly tabernacle.

Then he took the Book of the Covenant and read it in the hearing of the people. And they said, "All that the LORD has spoken we will do, and we will be obedient." **And Moses took the blood and threw it** on the people and said, "Behold the blood of the covenant that the LORD has made with you in accordance with all these words." (Ex. 24:7–8)

For when every commandment of the law had been declared by Moses to all the people, he took the blood of calves and goats, with water and scarlet wool and hyssop, and sprinkled both the book itself and all the people, saying, "This is the blood of the covenant that God commanded for you." And in the same way **he sprinkled with the blood** both the tent and all the vessels used in worship. Indeed, under the law almost everything is purified with blood, and without the shedding of blood there is no forgiveness of sins. (Heb. 9:19–22)

In the Old Covenant, the people of God were consecrated and set apart by various means. This sprinkling of blood was one of them.

Therefore I will divide him a portion with the many, and he shall divide the spoil with the strong, because he poured out his soul to death and was numbered with the transgressors; yet he **bore the sin of many**, and makes intercession for the transgressors. (Is. 53:12)

So Christ, having been offered once **to bear the sins of many**, will appear a second time, not to deal with sin but to save those who are eagerly waiting for him. (Heb. 9:28)

The great prophecy of the sacrifice of Christ in Isaiah 53 is alluded to multiple times in the New Testament. The vicarious death of Christ was for many; he died in their stead, bearing their sins. The clear teaching of Isaiah reinforces what theologians call penal substitution—and the writer of Hebrews echoes the same theme here.

In sacrifice and offering you have not delighted, but you have given me an open ear. Burnt offering and sin offering you have not required. Then I said, "Behold, I have come; in the scroll of the book it is written of me: I delight to do your will, O my God; your law is within my heart." (Ps. 40:6–8; "a body hast thou prepared me," LXX.)

Consequently, when Christ came into the world, he said, "**Sacrifices and offerings you have not desired, but a body have you prepared for me; in burnt offerings and sin offerings you have taken no pleasure. Then I said, 'Behold, I have come to do your will, O God, as it is written of me in the scroll of the book.**' " When he said above, "**You have neither desired nor taken pleasure in sacrifices and offerings and burnt offerings and sin offerings**" (these are offered according to the law), then he added, "Behold, I have come to do your will." He does away with the first in order to establish the second. And by that will we have been sanctified through the offering of the body of Jesus Christ once for all. (Heb. 10:5–10)

The chief interest here is in the difference between "a body you have prepared for me" and "you have given me an open ear," which is the rendering of the Hebrew Old Testament. The question would be how did "you have given me an open ear" turn into "a body you have prepared for me"? A reasonable question, with the most reasonable answer being that the reference to the ears is a reference to a person's body being set apart as the body of a slave when his ear was pierced by an awl at his master's house (Ex. 21:6).

The LORD says to my Lord: "**Sit at my right hand**, until I make your enemies your footstool." (Ps. 110:1)

But when Christ had offered for all time a single sacrifice for sins, **he sat down at the right hand of God.** (Heb. 10:12)

We have yet another reference to the royal edict in Psalm 110.

"**But this is the covenant that I will make** with the house of Israel **after those days, declares the LORD: I will put my law within them, and I will write it on their hearts**. And I will be their God, and they shall be my people. And no longer shall each one teach his neighbor and each his brother, saying, 'Know the LORD,' for they shall all know me, from the least of them to the greatest, declares the LORD. For **I will forgive their iniquity, and I will remember their sin no more.**" (Jer. 31:33–34)

"**This is the covenant that I will make** with them **after those days, declares the Lord: I will put my laws on their hearts, and write them on their minds," then he adds, "I will remember their sins and their lawless deeds no more.**" (Heb. 10:16–17)

This is the second citation of Jeremiah 31, in abridged form. The key terms of the New Covenant are the placing of the law in our "inward parts," and the full and complete forgiveness of sins.

On the evidence of two witnesses or of three witnesses the one who is to die shall be put to death; a person shall not be put to death on the evidence of one witness. (Deut. 17:6).

Anyone who has set aside the law of Moses **dies** without mercy **on the evidence of two or three witnesses.** (Heb. 10:28)

This is one of the fundamental requirements of biblical law. No one is to be convicted on the testimony of a solitary witness. But when two or three witnesses lined up, the punishment could be severe. The argument in Hebrews is *a fortiori*—how much *more* will those who despise the New Covenant be subject to punishment—especially in light of the great cloud of *witnesses* coming up in the next chapter.

Then he took the Book of the Covenant and read it in the hearing of the people. And they said, "All that the LORD has spoken we will do, and we will be obedient." **And Moses took the blood** and threw it on the people **and said, "Behold the blood of the covenant** that the LORD has made with you in accordance with all these words." (Ex. 24:7–8)

How much worse punishment, do you think, will be deserved by the one who has spurned the Son of God, and has profaned the **blood of the covenant by which he was sanctified**, and has outraged the Spirit of grace? (Heb. 10:29)

This passage, along with many others, shows that God sets his covenant people aside in the same basic way in the time of the New Covenant. We have a remarkable tendency to draw contrasts between the Old and New Covenants at just the places where the biblical writers are drawing parallels. The Old Testament saints were set apart or sanctified by the blood of the covenant, as are the New Testament saints. Some of these objective saints (in both covenants) fall away, and condemn the blood of the covenant. None of the elect can fall away, but members of the covenant (anywhere in the Bible) most certainly can.

For still the vision awaits its appointed time; it hastens to the end—it will not lie. If it seems slow, wait for it; **it will surely come; it will not delay**. "Behold, his soul is puffed up; it is not upright within him, but **the righteous shall live by his faith.**" (Hab. 2:3–4)

For, "Yet a little while, and the coming one will come and will not delay." (Heb. 10:37)

The famous passage (the righteous shall live by his faith) is given by the prophet Habakkuk in the context of God's people longing for their promised salvation. They are assured that though it may *seem* to tarry, yet will it not *really* tarry. Hang on, in other words. Just a few verses later, the prophet promised that the "earth will be filled with the knowledge of the glory of the LORD as the waters cover the sea" (Hab. 2:14). And now the generation receiving this epistle to the Hebrews is just a few months from the beginning of that great fulfillment. It is doubly important for them to hang on.

And Abel also brought of the firstborn of his flock and of their fat portions. And the **LORD had regard for Abel** and his offering. (Gen. 4:4)

By faith **Abel offered to God a more acceptable sacrifice** than Cain, through which he was commended as righteous, **God commending him by accepting his gifts**. And through his faith, though he died, he still speaks. (Heb. 11:4)

Genesis tells us that Abel offered blood sacrifices and the fat offering from his flock. Hebrews tells us that this was a more excellent sacrifice.

Enoch walked with God after he fathered Methuselah 300 years and had other sons and daughters. Thus all the days of Enoch were 365 years. **Enoch walked with God**, and he was not, for **God took him.** (Gen. 5:22–24)

By faith Enoch was taken up so that he should not see death, and he was not found, **because God had taken him**. Now before he was taken he was commended as **having pleased God.** (Heb. 11:5)

This is not a direct citation, but it is a very clear summary of what Genesis said about Enoch.

Now the LORD said to Abram, "Go from your country and your kindred and your father's house **to the land that I will show you**. And I will make of you a great nation, and I

By faith **Abraham** obeyed when he was called to go out to a place that he was to receive as an inheritance. And he **went out, not knowing where he was going.** (Heb. 11:8)

will bless you and make your name great, so that you will be a blessing. I will bless those who bless you, and him who dishonors you I will curse, and in you all the families of the earth shall be blessed." **So Abram went**, as the LORD had told him, and Lot went with him. Abram was seventy-five years old when he departed from Haran. (Gen. 12:1–4)

The passage in Genesis tells us that God told Abraham that he would tell him later what his destination was. The writer of Hebrews infers from this, rightly enough, that Abraham did not know where he was going when he left. He departed from his home country in faith.

And Abraham rose up from before his dead and said to the Hittites, "**I am a sojourner and foreigner among you**; give me property among you for a burying place, that I may bury my dead out of my sight." (Gen. 23:3–4)

By faith he went to live in the land of promise, **as in a foreign land**, living in tents with Isaac and Jacob, heirs with him of the same promise. (Heb. 11:9)

He came to the land that was promised to him, and to his descendants, but he did not set down permanent roots—he did not build a city, in other words. Abraham dwelt in tents, even though the residents of the land around him dwelt in cities. He understood himself to be a pilgrim there ("I am a sojourner and foreigner"), and this is how Hebrews speaks of him as well, as dwelling "as in a foreign land."

And the angel of the LORD called to Abraham a second time from heaven and said, "By myself I have sworn, declares the LORD, because you have done this and have not withheld your son, your only son, I

Therefore from one man, and him as good as dead, were born descendants **as many as the stars of heaven and as many as the innumerable grains of sand by the seashore.** (Heb. 11:12)

will surely bless you, and I will surely multiply your offspring **as the stars of heaven and as the sand that is on the seashore**. And your offspring shall possess the gate of his enemies, and in your offspring shall all the nations of the earth be blessed, because you have obeyed my voice." (Gen. 22:15–18)

"Please deliver me from the hand of my brother, from the hand of Esau, for I fear him, that he may come and attack me, the mothers with the children. But you said, 'I will surely do you good, **and make your offspring as the sand of the sea, which cannot be numbered for multitude**'." (Gen. 32:11–12)

God told Abraham that he would have countless descendants—like the stars in the sky, or like the grains of sand on the beach. This promise was handed down through Isaac, and came in the third generation to Jacob, who cites the promise as well. The writer of Hebrews boasts in the fulfillment of that promise from Abraham, from one "as good as dead."

And Abraham rose up from before his dead and said to the Hittites, "**I am a sojourner and foreigner among you**; give me property among you for a burying place, that I may bury my dead out of my sight." (Gen. 23:3–4)

These all died in faith, not having received the things promised, but having seen them and greeted them from afar, and having acknowledged that they **were strangers and exiles** on the earth. (Heb. 11:13)

Therefore David blessed the LORD in the presence of all the assembly. And David said: "Blessed are you, O LORD, the God of Israel our father, forever and ever. Yours, O

LORD, is the greatness and the power and the glory and the victory and the majesty, for all that is in the heavens and in the earth is yours. Yours is the kingdom, O LORD, and you are exalted as head above all. Both riches and honor come from you, and you rule over all. In your hand are power and might, and in your hand it is to make great and to give strength to all. And now we thank you, our God, and praise your glorious name. "But who am I, and what is my people, that we should be able thus to offer willingly? For all things come from you, and of your own have we given you. **For we are strangers before you and sojourners, as all our fathers were**. Our days on the earth are like a shadow, and there is no abiding." (1 Chron. 29:10–15)

Not only was Abraham a stranger in the land of Palestine, but this was clearly a type of all earthly sojourning. All the Old Testament saints confessed themselves to be strangers and pilgrims on the earth. Abraham, living as a nomad, confessed this, but so did David, and he dwelt in the palace as king.

After these things God tested Abraham and said to him, "Abraham!" And he said, "Here am I." He said, "Take your son, **your only son Isaac**, whom you love, and go to the land of Moriah, and offer him there as a burnt offering on one of the mountains of which I shall tell you." So Abraham rose early in the morning, saddled his donkey, and took two of his young men with

By faith **Abraham**, when he was tested, **offered up Isaac**, and he who had received the promises was in the act of **offering up his only son**, of whom it was said, "Through Isaac shall your offspring be named." (Heb. 11:17–18)

> him, and his son Isaac. And he cut the wood for the burnt offering and arose and went to the place of which God had told him. On the third day Abraham lifted up his eyes and saw the place from afar. Then Abraham said to his young men, "Stay here with the donkey; I and the boy will go over there and worship and come again to you." And Abraham took the wood of the burnt offering and laid it on Isaac his son. And he took in his hand the fire and the knife. So they went both of them together. And Isaac said to his father Abraham, "My father!" And he said, "Here am I, my son." He said, "Behold, the fire and the wood, but where is the lamb for a burnt offering?" Abraham said, "God will provide for himself the lamb for a burnt offering, my son." So they went both of them together. When they came to the place of which God had told him, Abraham built the altar there and laid the wood in order and bound Isaac his son and laid him on the altar, on top of the wood. **Then Abraham reached out his hand and took the knife to slaughter his son.** (Gen. 22:1–10)

The point here cannot be emphasized too much or too frequently. The command to slay Isaac was not a test of Abraham's love for God. It was a test of his faith. This citation makes this point very plain. He that received the promises—that is, that in Isaac your seed will be called—was willing to sacrifice Isaac, because he knew that he was going to come back down off the mountain *with Isaac*, not with Isaac's body.

And when the time drew near that Israel must die, he called his son Joseph and said to him, "If now I have found favor in your sight, put your hand under my thigh and promise to deal kindly and truly with me. Do not bury me in Egypt, but let me lie with my fathers. Carry me out of Egypt and bury me in their burying place." He answered, "I will do as you have said." And he said, "Swear to me"; and he swore to him. Then Israel bowed himself upon the head of his bed. (Gen. 47:29–31)

". . . and **Israel worshipped upon the top of his staff.**" (Gen. 47:31, LXX)

By faith Jacob, when dying, blessed each of the sons of Joseph, **bowing in worship over the head of his staff.** (Heb. 11:21)

Here the writer to the Hebrews is quoting the Septuagint, and uses the alternative reading which says that Israel (Jacob) worshipped while leaning on his staff.

Now a man from the house of Levi went and took as his wife a Levite woman. The woman conceived and bore a son, **and when she saw that he was a fine child, she hid him three months.** (Ex. 2:1–2)

By faith Moses, when he was born, **was hidden for three months by his parents, because they saw that the child was beautiful**, and they were not afraid of the king's edict. (Heb. 11:23)

By faith the parents of Moses engaged in a little civil disobedience, disregarding the Reproductive Services and Demography Act.

One day, **when Moses had grown** up, he went out to his people and looked on their burdens, and he saw an Egyptian beating a Hebrew, one of his people. He looked this way and that, and seeing no one, he

By faith **Moses, when he was grown up**, refused to be called the son of Pharaoh's daughter, choosing rather to be mistreated with the people of God than to enjoy the fleeting pleasures of sin. (Heb. 11:24–25)

struck down the Egyptian and hid him in the sand. (Ex. 2:11–12)

Hebrews here settles the question of whether Moses was sinning when he struck the Egyptian. Referring to this time, Hebrews tells us that Moses did what he did "by faith."

Remember, O Lord, how your servants are mocked, and how I bear in my heart the insults of all the many nations, with which your enemies mock, O LORD, with which they mock the footsteps of your anointed. Blessed be the LORD forever! Amen and Amen. (Ps. 89:50–52)

For zeal for your house has consumed me, **and the reproaches of those who reproach you have fallen on me.** (Ps. 69:9)

He considered the reproach of Christ greater wealth than the treasures of Egypt, for he was looking to the reward. (Heb. 11:26)

The Messiah fell under the reproach of men long before he was born, and Moses saw that reproach and resolved to share in it.

Then Moses called all the elders of Israel and said to them, "Go and select lambs for yourselves according to your clans, and kill the Passover lamb. Take a bunch of hyssop and dip it in the blood that is in the basin, and **touch the lintel and the two doorposts with the blood that is in the basin**. None of you shall go out of the door of his house until the morning. For the LORD will pass through to strike the Egyptians, and when he sees the blood on the lintel and on the two doorposts, the LORD will pass over the door and will not allow the destroyer to enter your

By faith he left Egypt . . . By faith **he kept the Passover and sprinkled the blood**, so that the Destroyer of the firstborn might not touch them. (Heb. 11:27–28)

houses to strike you. You shall observe this rite as a statute for you and for your sons forever. And when you come to the land that the LORD will give you, as he has promised, you shall keep this service. And when your children say to you, 'What do you mean by this service?' you shall say, 'It is the sacrifice of the LORD's Passover, for he passed over the houses of the people of Israel in Egypt, when he struck the Egyptians but spared our houses.' " And the people bowed their heads and worshiped. Then the people of Israel went and did so; as the LORD had commanded Moses and Aaron, so they did. At midnight the LORD struck down all the firstborn in the land of Egypt, from the firstborn of Pharaoh who sat on his throne to the firstborn of the captive who was in the dungeon, and all the firstborn of the livestock. (Ex. 12:21–29)

When Moses kept the first Passover, sprinkling blood on the doorposts, thus protecting the first born sons of Israel, he did this by faith.

The LORD says to my Lord: "**Sit at my right hand**, until I make your enemies your footstool." (Ps 110:1)

Looking to Jesus, the founder and perfecter of our faith, who for the joy that was set before him endured the cross, despising the shame, **and is seated at the right hand** of the throne of God. (Heb. 12:2)

Again, the book of Hebrews makes a great deal out of where our king and priest is seated.

Strengthen the weak hands, and make firm the feeble knees. Say to those who have an anxious heart, "Be strong; fear not! Behold, your God will come with vengeance, with the recompense of God. He will come and save you." (Is. 35:3–4)	Therefore **lift your drooping hands and strengthen your weak knees.** (Heb. 12:12)

The first recipients of this letter were on the verge of giving up. Not only that, but they were going to give up right before the deliverance was going to come. They were near the finish line, and this kind of encouragement would do them a great deal of good. According to the context of Isaiah, God was just about to intervene on their behalf.

"**Make thou straight paths for thy feet** . . ." (Prov. 4:26, LXX)	And **make straight paths for your feet**, so that what is lame may not be put out of joint but rather be healed. (Heb. 12:13)

The same kind of encouragement continues in the same vein.

Turn away from evil and do good; **seek peace and pursue it.** (Ps. 34:14)	**Strive for peace with everyone**, and for the holiness without which no one will see the Lord. (Heb. 12:14)

While these Christians were longing for the great transition into the Christian era, they were to pursue peace with all men, and it wouldn't be easy.

"Is there among you **any root springing up in gall and bitterness?**" (Deut. 29:17–18, LXX)	See to it that no one fails to obtain the grace of God; that no "**root of bitterness**" **springs up and causes trouble**, and by it many become defiled. (Heb. 12:15)

In the context of this passage from Deuteronomy, the gall and bitterness is connected to idolatry. In the previous verse, the warning is explicitly tied to the problem of idolatry. "You know how we lived in the land of Egypt, and how we came through the midst of the nations through which you passed. And you have seen their detestable things, their idols of wood and stone, of silver and gold, which were among them"—and this means the New Testament passage should not be limited to a question of personal resentments. That does not mean personal resentments are not included, but rather that we should be careful to see them in the context of heart idolatry.

Jacob said, "Swear to me now." So he swore to him and **sold his birthright** to Jacob. Then Jacob gave Esau bread and lentil stew, and he ate and drank and rose and went his way. Thus Esau despised his birthright. (Gen. 25:33–34)

That no one is sexually immoral or unholy like **Esau**, who **sold his birthright for a single meal.** (Heb. 12:16)

The central sin that Esau committed was that of selling his birthright. And when Hebrews says that he could not find a way of repentance for that sin, it meant that he could not figure out a way to undo it—the consequences were settled.

And as soon as you heard the voice out of the midst of the darkness, while the mountain was burning with fire, you came near to me, all the heads of your tribes, and your elders. And you said, "Behold, the LORD our God has shown us his glory and greatness, and we have heard his voice out of the midst of the fire. This day we have seen **God speak with man, and man still live. Now therefore why should we die? For this great fire will consume us. If we hear the voice of the LORD our God any more, we shall die.**" (Deut. 5:23–25)

And **the sound of a trumpet and a voice whose words made the hearers beg that no further messages be spoken to them.** (Heb. 12:19)

On the morning of the third day there were thunders and lightnings and a thick cloud on the mountain and a **very loud trumpet blast**, so that all the people in the camp trembled. (Ex. 19:16)

In the older covenant, the people of God were afraid of the voice of God and shrank back—lest they be destroyed. In the New Covenant, the destruction happens if the people *do* shrink back.

And you shall set limits for the people all around, saying, "Take care not to go up into the mountain or touch the edge of it. **Whoever touches the mountain shall be put to death.**" (Ex. 19:12)

For they could not endure the order that was given, "**If even a beast touches the mountain, it shall be stoned.**" (Heb. 12:20)

The Old Covenant was made in a way calculated to make the people realize the utter holiness of God. In the New Covenant that holiness has not evaporated, but rather is settled in Jesus, the high priest in the order of Melchizedek, seated at the right hand of God.

For I was afraid of the anger and hot displeasure that the LORD bore against you, so that he was ready to destroy you. But the LORD listened to me that time also. (Deut. 9:19)

Indeed, so terrifying was the sight that Moses said, "**I tremble with fear.**" (Heb. 12:21)

Overt fear was the appropriate response to the manifestation of God at Sinai.

"For thus says the LORD of hosts: **Yet once more, in a little while, I will shake the heavens and the earth and the sea and the dry land**. And I will shake all nations, so that the treasures of all nations shall come in, and I will fill this house

At that time his voice shook the **earth, but now he has promised, "Yet once more I will shake not only the earth but also the heavens**." This phrase, "Yet once more," indicates the removal of things that are shaken—that is, things that with glory, says the LORD of hosts. The silver is mine, and the gold is mine, declares the LORD of hosts. The latter glory of this house shall be greater than the former, says the LORD of hosts. And in this place I will give peace, declares the LORD of hosts." (Hag. 2:6–9)

have been made—in order that the things that cannot be shaken may remain. (Heb. 12:26–27)

The contrast that is being set up is an *a fortiori* one, in favor of the New Covenant. In other words, it is not that the Old Covenant was terrifying, and that now in the New Covenant God has calmed down. Rather, God was terrifying in the Old Covenant, and now in the New Covenant, the right kind of fear ascends even higher. At Sinai, God shook the earth. In the worship of the heavenly Zion, God shakes both earth *and* heaven, in accordance with the words of Haggai the prophet.

Take care, lest you forget the covenant of the LORD your God, which he made with you, and make a carved image, . . . **For the LORD your God is a consuming fire**, a jealous God. (Deut. 4:24)

For **our God is a consuming fire.** (Heb. 12:29)

Again, it is not that God was a consuming fire in the Old Covenant, but that now in the New, the fire has gone out. Rather, God is a jealous God always.

Out of my distress I called on the LORD; the LORD answered me and set me free. **The LORD is on my side; I will not fear. What can man do to me?** (Ps. 118:6)

So we can confidently say, "**The Lord is my helper; I will not fear; what can man do to me?**" (Heb. 13:6)

The encouragement that is offered, in both testaments, is encouragement for the conflict. The book of Hebrews was written to

Christians who were beginning to waver in the conflict. And so this psalm is quoted, and reapplied.

And the bull for the sin offering and the goat for the sin offering, whose blood was brought in to make atonement in the Holy Place, **shall be carried outside the camp. Their skin and their flesh and their dung shall be burned up with fire.** (Lev. 16:27)

For the bodies of those animals whose blood is brought into the holy places by the high priest as a sacrifice for sin are burned outside the camp. So Jesus also suffered outside the gate in order to sanctify the people through his own blood. Therefore let us go to him **outside the camp and bear the reproach he endured.** (Heb. 13:11–13)

The sacrifices had two places in Israel—one was at the center, at the temple. The other was outside the city, where the sacrificial refuse was disposed of. Jesus was the antitype of this type when he was executed outside the city.

"If I were hungry, I would not tell you, for the world and its fullness are mine. Do I eat the flesh of bulls or drink the blood of goats? **Offer to God a sacrifice of thanksgiving**, and perform your vows to the Most High, and call upon me in the day of trouble; I will deliver you, and you shall glorify me." (Ps. 50:12–15)

If he offers it for a thanksgiving, **then he shall offer with the thanksgiving sacrifice** unleavened loaves mixed with oil, unleavened wafers smeared with oil, and loaves of fine flour well mixed with oil. (Lev. 7:12)

Through him then let us continually **offer up a sacrifice of praise to God**, that is, the fruit of lips that acknowledge his name. (Heb. 13:15)

The book of Hebrews clearly teaches us that blood sacrifices are done for good because of the once-for-all sacrifice of Christ on the cross. No more of that. But this does not remove the language of sacrifice—all of that is picked up in the musical worship of the church.

". . . creating the **fruit of the lips**. Peace, peace, to the far and to the near," says the LORD, "and I will heal him." (Is. 57:19)

Return, O Israel, to the LORD your God, for you have stumbled because of your iniquity. Take with you words and return to the LORD; say to him, "Take away all iniquity; accept what is good, and **we will pay with bulls the vows of our lips."** (Hos. 14:1–2)

Through him then let us continually offer up a sacrifice of praise to God, that is, the **fruit of lips that acknowledge his name.** (Heb. 13:15)

In addition to the music of praise, we also offer the fruit of our lips, whether in prayers, thanksgiving, readings, or preaching. Such things are also offered up to God in the New Covenant ascension offering.

Then he remembered the days of old, of Moses and his people. Where is he who brought them up out of the sea with the **shepherds of his flock**? Where is he who put in the midst of them his Holy Spirit, who caused his glorious arm to go at the right hand of Moses, who divided the waters before them to make for himself an everlasting name? (Is. 63:11–12)

Now may the God of peace who brought again from the dead our Lord Jesus, the **great shepherd of the sheep**, by the blood of the eternal covenant. (Heb. 13:20)

The Lord is our Shepherd, we shall not want.

Incline your ear, and come to me; hear, that your soul may live; and I will make with you an **everlasting**

Now may the God of peace who brought again from the dead our Lord Jesus, the great shepherd of

covenant, my steadfast, sure love for David. (Is. 55:3)

Rejoice greatly, O daughter of Zion! Shout aloud, O daughter of Jerusalem! Behold, your king is coming to you; righteous and having salvation is he, humble and mounted on a donkey, on a colt, the foal of a donkey. I will cut off the chariot from Ephraim and the war horse from Jerusalem; and the battle bow shall be cut off, and he shall speak peace to the nations; his rule shall be from sea to sea, and from the River to the ends of the earth. As for you also, because of the **blood of my covenant with you**, I will set your prisoners free from the waterless pit. (Zech. 9:9–11)

I will make a covenant of peace with them. **It shall be an everlasting covenant with them**. And I will set them in their land and multiply them, and will set my sanctuary in their midst forevermore. (Ez. 37:26)

the sheep, by the blood of the **eternal covenant** . . . (Heb. 13:20)

God made a promise to Abraham that encompassed the entire history of the world. It was an everlasting covenant. That means the coming of Christ did not abrogate what God had told Abraham, but rather fulfilled it.